Primera Página

Poetry from the Latino Heartland

2nd Edition

Primera Página

Poetry from the Latino Heartland

2nd Edition

Latino Writers Collective

Kansas City

with a preface by Rane Arroyo

Cucui Press

Kansas City, Missouri

Cover art: *Nagual #1* by Maria Vasquez Boyd
The collective wishes to thank Gabriela N. Lemmons, Dale A. Lemmons, Eloisa Pérez-Lozano, Ben Furnish, Xánath Caraza and Patricio H. Lazen.
Proceeds from this book will benefit the collective's community outreach programs.

Latino Writers Collective
The Writers Place
3607 Pennsylvania Avenue
Kansas City, Missouri 64111
latinowriters@gmail.com
www.latinowriterscollective.com

Cucui Press
3607 Pennslyvania Avenue
Kansas City, Missouri 64111
cucuipress@gmail.com

Primera Página: Poetry from the Latino Heartland - 2nd Edition/ The Latino Writers Collective, Kansas City; with a preface by Rane Arroyo.

ISBN-10: 0-9895844-0-2

ISBN-13: 978-0-9895844-0-1

ACKNOWLEDGEMENTS

The following poems appeared first in these publications.

"the movement: freestyles for the dying sun," "mission redux," and "cuando ganamos" (Tomás Riley): *Mahcic* (Calaca Press)

"Chronicle of a Salvadoran Girl" and "El Gritón" (Andrés Rodríguez): *Bilingual Review*

"Malinche on Cortés" (Andrés Rodríguez), "Kooties" (Angela Cervantes), "Brown Eyes in Blues" (Chato Villalobos), and "La Trenza" (Gabriela N. Lemmons): *Kansas City Hispanic News*

"Sin Calzón" (Gabriela N. Lemmons): *Just Like a Girl: A Manifesta!* (Girlchild Press)

"Tía Licha's House" (Gustavo Adolfo Aybar): *Number One*

"Blame It On Summer" and "Considering Oceans" (Linda Rodriguez): *Skin Hunger* (Potpourri Publications).

"Brown Eyes in Blues" (Chato Villalobos), "Buñuelos," "Kansas," "Sin Calzón," (Gabriela N. Lemmons), "Mis Mil y Una Noches" (Gustavo Adolfo Aybar), "Calaca Comedy Central," "Making Enchiladas," "The Things She Gave Me" and "Ghosts" (Linda Rodriguez): *Present Magazine*

"Lydia's Phantasmagoria" and "new shoes and an old flame" (Gloria Vando): *Shadows & Supposes* (Arte de Público Press)

CONTENTS

Preface: The Here in Where

1.

Latinos are unusually associated with geography: the Caribbean, south of the U.S. border, Miami, New York, the Southwest and southern California, for example. It turns out that in the American Heartlands, el corazón de este país, there are many of us Latinos—from various genealogies—thriving, struggling and, most importantly for this project, writing.

2.

But why poetry? Why not write novels with narratives that deal with Americanization issues or that re-create the contexts within which we come to claim our complex identities? Or publish creative non-fiction works that detail personal struggles and some triumphs against the odds of the survival of our cultural integrity? Poetry understands poverty, oppression, joy, music, and is never ashamed by our nakedness. It is also portable when it is read often enough and/or committed to memory. Rhythm and images in this anthology offer a codex.

3.

How might Latino poets living in the Midwest differ from those writing and living in other parts of our country? Read these poets for that answer. Follow them as they discover and detonate specific places, popular culture objects like Barbie (the doll used to Americanize Latinas), gang wars in absurdly non-critical turfs, love, and of course, the family with its offers of safety and danger. Their words wear the landscape of green, flatness, cornfields, cities abandoned by corporations, and inland beauty. Context informs these texts.

4.

Primera Página, or the first page, the start of the story or book of poems, the invitation to the reader to go to the second and other pages, is well-named. This is a major first anthology of Latinos in a collective who both accept and defy their identities. I grew up without an anthology of this and had to imagine it. Now the book is here and I feel less and less invisible about the value of my experiences and insights. The first shall be first, sometimes. I also hear the word primavera, Spring, the season of the future being realized.

5.

In the poem "Prayer Before Meals," a brief family portrait, Jennifer Prado declares, without ambiguity or ego, that "I'm going to eat the world." Yes, this is an anthology about hunger and negotiation.

6.

Many of us writers who are different because of sexual orientation, skin color, mixed-culture backgrounds, physical abilities, gender or other typologies end up in an intense conversation with the (perceived) majority: our observations about our life prove that we are not anyone's mirror. Reading these poems, I'm struck by how each poet sounds unique despite sharing the common language of disaffection. Some poets are young while others have scars from several decades ago. Yet there is a common wisdom shared among them, the collective, about how each voice must be heard on its own terms. This book is not a choir, but rather a gathering of singers offering world music.

7.

In my own career, I've been often encouraged to head to "one of the coasts" in order to establish my life as a writer. I've tried it, several times, but always seem to return to the Midwest where I was born. I had to learn to embrace my identity as a Midwest writer, that it was here where I learned to be culturally bilingual. These poets are fluent in that sense of place and displacement.

8.

I encourage the reader to read these poems aloud. These are not echoes, but the originating voices of echoes.

9.

In "The Name Of The Grandfather," the poet Andrés Rodríguez says simply, "That old story is always worth repeating." He is right. Also, though, each story is made new by the telling and by the tellers. The poets here seem to grasp the importance of linking the past to the future and that the immediate plays a key role in preserving stories, poems, and prayers.

10.

What an honor it is for me to be invited to write this preface. I look forward to the growth of these poets as national voices while trusting that they never forget the Midwest, the land of scarecrows and winds speaking Spanish fluently.

Rane Arroyo

Tomás Riley was one of the original Taco Shop Poets in southern California. He agreed to be the Latino Writers Collective's guest reader at Primera Página, our first reading series. When we were just getting started, he came to Kansas City to help us (without a guarantee of fee), not only by reading his fine work in our series but by hanging out with us and telling us wise stories of his experience with that earlier collective that was so influential in Latino literature. We are pleased that he has agreed to be our special guest poet in this anthology.

the movement: freestyles for the dying sun

movement
march
panzón to guitarrón
and liquified p-funk
maintain
norteños mas allá
vicente fernandez
chilling in his b-boy stance
talking trash about
"que de raro tiene"
          no
es más raro que tenemos
tony lamas
timbos
tripping
ain't no half stepping
in the movement

mariachi muse(sic) riffs
against the twilight
of an olmec head nod
hands fly
flecha fast
to dominate the plate
rotating in the dark
obsidian
outcast on the remix
overrun
by selva sagrada
con su machete
en la mano
mascarada

"nosotros,
hombres y mujeres
íntegros y libres,
estamos conscientes

de que la guerra que declaramos
es una medida última
pero justa"

but don't call it a comeback
we still got mobs of modern macehuales
moving
at the acceleration of gravity
meditating on the microcosm
of the 12-inch
buried mirrors
more than they can stand
who-riding
in a county van

movement
in the middle of caras perdidas
homenaje
al pasaje
suroeste
where pilot pens
don't take to vinyl
where they need
to draw the line
where the morning left
a midnight of our migration
on a dance floor

damn,
you mean there's four sacred directions
and all that ceremony shit?
yo, i might have to

take two and pass
take two and pass
take two and pass
won't get off my ass

the movement
finds a moment in repose
a mass

unanswered prayer
of signs and sirens
break beats
booming off a red sun
caught
between the upkeep
and the downstroke
movimiento
or moving momentos
on a 45
waxing
oh-no-myth-opaeic
when the needle hits the groove
old heads still
bouncing to the bank
close to the real estate

movement
spins 360
freeze
let the beat drop
into uprock
leaning
toward the center
of ciphers come lately
flair kick
scissor slicing
hooded heads
with ash
and empty bottles
running
off the r.p.m.

movement
measured in the line length
of a freestyle
for the dying sun
a rough face
leapt into the lyric
ticking
tongue glyphs

up the temple steps
rhyme
from reed songs
rolling
to the east
my brother
to the east

where the whole house
bounce to rooftops
and the sky
begins
brand new

so you can
throw your hands to the sky
and wave em
from side to side
but if you came here
to spark up the movement, y'all
you better get here
fo' the whole thing dies

mission redux

mission manifesto made redux
reprise
re-use
mash on
an under-echelon
of epitaphs
made murals

tore down
our niche beneath potrero
on a smokestack colored morning
and the children
off to school
there was a bell
teacher remembers
antiseptic anthems
over antithetic rubrics
and better still
the children come
on foot
with infantile arrogance
they come
with tablets and with pencils
empty baskets
built for hesitation
built for limbs etched out
in light and concrete
wounds
replace the wombs
of mother's lungs
exquisite time
on tongues
cut taken
this ephemera
that shimmers
on the glassy eyes of children
running

raging
into no one's dying light
beyond the clasping of their lashes
shutting out
the flowing visions
of shared bedrooms
and a dusty kitchen table

these
they will not sacrifice
as lids grip tighter
over memory and place
displaced
the new beginnings
of old endings
where the stop and go days
last longer
than the curse of shattered mirrors
dreams
reflected of themselves
retreating
into multiplicity
made history
of hunger
and invisible arms
locked into barely felt embrace
a face
that time will never know
seeking
over ever-present mounds
from last night's eviction
cast off
by many mourners
holding hands
maintaining ranks
solidified by
silence

somedays
the children

reach out
on paper white shirtsleeves
trailing blue bandera uniforms
through cancer causing breeze
so many
kites without tails
sin ganas de volar
emerging wings
already clipped
become the fall
of western wal mart
ridden
by the complex schemes
of 99¢ shopping
on the lowlands
of a highbrow culture

mission manifesto
made redux
reprise
re-use
mash on
the under-echelon
of epitaphs
made murals
on mission street
at noon
between the traffic cones
and overdue construction
beyond the solace of a bus bench
girl goes pushing
pushing into sweaty days
jalando
tres generaciones
wearing faded chivas jersey
the markers
more the milestones
have moved so far
from making sense
because she

cannot speak the language
she just
looks with rage
imbedded within
the inability to look
to sing
the song and psalms of looking
at ourselves
in equal measure
we see buddha
and ritchie valens

call them scars
as we been tongue lashed
through the ages
the first word
become an epilogue
forbidden
from the dialogue
we marinate
on tax breaks
watching weary arms
tow children
toward september
when school begins
and language
becomes pretense
disaggregate delusion
a satchel we keep tugging
through television windows
like linguistic thieves at night
ready to pocket the silver
and render
english
unto caesar

born
with the sun
in our mouths
become a hummingbird swarm

pinned
to the collar of an unwashed shirt
like a note
sent home from teacher
bearing
the standards
like illuminated manuscripts
kids read
only
the pictures
wringing palabras from
soaking garments
straight white-washed
in the translation
but hanging on the line
we fail
only
the children

isn't it all
just so
familiar?
how even
their silence
has a vibration
how rhetoric
subsides?
how in the interim
we pause
and hold our breath
over millennia?

one thousand one
one thousand two
one thousand three

cuando ganamos

shadows of the new forreal
fall sixty stories
over antique row apartments
where victoria runs crooked
under late victorians

dipping from the sloping sun
making room
for undone renovations
and the sprawl
of this new street
maintaining
life
above its own

your town
my town
anytown usa

there's no
new
here
no
viable
no
cradle of the crescent
only
after-school unrest
a rumored peace
without
the decency
of truthtelling

we
armed only
with obsessions for silence
and for waving hands
say

get your hands up
get your hands in the air
but can't stop
the double-dip parlays
at the corner stores
where the homies chill
in lawn chairs
the unknown warriors
that lean
un
steadily
against a mural
of their own fifth sun

as if we'd need a reason
to subdue the urges
of our exodus
the exegesis
spilling
onto sidewalks
where the old gods
are remembered
and you just
can't step there blood

this said
through telepathic logic
and the passing of a paper bag
where we spit
40-ounce foam,
and roll up
on the unsuspecting destiny
of power lines
and patrol cars
ever clocking
as the world
has shrunk to
this

from the moment we left dreaming
left with
leering sadness
sleeping
on street corners
stoops
have stooped too low
enduring the weight
of everyday absolution

in the poem
we must name
the hottest corners
that we've been through
this
the willing traces
of our pens
across the pavement
corners
leaning
against lampposts
where the malos
carry on with markers
at artilleries
of old strategic planning
and the myths
that are good citizens
have taken their good will
toward our center
we see
socrates
holding a vial
at 24th and mission

where the mangoes
drip from traffic lights
grown weary
in the haze of grey saturdays
and pulsing cars

line up
to start the plucking
at the intersection

those on foot survey
so many rows of luggage racks
lining sidewalks
for a population bent
on traveling home

always departing
as they arrive
in ten dollar duffel bags
with pockets lined
with telegiros
and lotto tickets
scratching
at the chances
for return

a una isla encantada
a una montaña en centroamerica
a un rancho lindo y lejos
de este pueblo congelado

unreachable
those mangoes
should the traffic lights
through civic sympathy or shame
allow their frozen fruit
to fall at 24th street
we would dive
within the skin and pulp
before they even
hit the pavement
beyond the fleshy fiber strands
the meat
beyond original confusion
we would fight

to find the pit of fruitless searches
for beginnings
but fruit's not gonna fall
and sympathetic poets
don't fertilize fool
and you ain't growin no trees

bueno mano
si quieres mangos
vamos al chinito buey

so we hit the spot
pop the top
on nectars come in cans
like the essence
that is us-sense
chillin in the coolers
of chinito's corner store
where old drunks
slanted sideways
on a $50 million jackpot dream
play lotto
and complain about
la renta

they'll take their crumpled tickets home tonight
the numbers plucked
from memories and shame
tonight
someone behind a tv tray
within a damp apartment
will tune in to anticipate
the call of
birthdates
children's ages
days since their arrival
street addresses
fake social security numbers
saints days
bible passages

years when they were happy
and even those will not appear
will not deliver
out their random race through time
toward the going back
to leave them
quietly needing
in the dark

bueno mano
cuando ganamos
compramos mangos

damn that bro
if we win
i'm buyin you
some mangoes

CHRONICLE OF A SALVADORAN GIRL

from the Spanish of José Roberto Cea

When I met her—
and pardon me for saying so—
she was a peach.
Any man could gobble her up just by looking,
or strip her little by little
of dress and modesty
till she was naked, helpless.

She was always
that same content, smiling girl,
at her ease and full of life.
Some women were jealous of her charm,
others proud that one of their own
set so high an example.

When I met her,
she went to high school, to basketball games,
read the society news in the paper
and Red Pillow romance novels.
Well, yes, she dreamed.
She built her castles in the air
and had a blue prince who loved her.
(Blue was her word for love.)
She went to dances, wishing she'd drop her slipper
and was thrilled seeing a yellow Jag
slicing the air as it passed.
She wore tight sweaters to show her hot little tits
and pencil skirts to show off her ass.

Her story is terrible.

When I met her,
she liked to hear the come-ons of the homeboys
and the bold music of their whistles.

She went through the streets like a champ,
too great even to fit on the sidewalk.

The whole city watched her,
and no one knew she existed.
She crossed parks, porticoes, plazas, window-shopping.
She smiled, buying happiness wholesale.
She surpassed fortune, smiled again, and turned homeward.
The neighbors loved her, hated her, sighed for her.
Again they placed her nude over the tender grass of desire.
It was finally something marvelous
having her at pointblank range.

Her story is terrible and ordinary.

It was easy to know her,
wear her like a boutonniere,
show her off to preppy girls,
to boys who cheat on their exams,
and those who yank off in public johns,
hell, even to dirty old men who dye their hair,
all those filthy, lying codgers who have
no country, no leader, no god at all.

This girl's case is common.

When I met her, she never really cried,
except for a couple of tantrums crowned with tears,
and once when something got in her eyes.

What a girl after our own heart!
What loveliness! What aimlessness!

Enough of that.

But what a Christian child!
What tender veal for sale!

I saw her. I felt for her.
I pushed her. I left her.
We have her.

There she is
among desires without streets,

among obscene words,
among old geezers in cheap wigs,
among rendezvous in hip joints,
among jobs that yield no lovers,
among dried up, frustrated bosses,
among shadows that grow colder, deeper in anguish,
among rumors that never speak a word of truth
and looks that never speak at all . . .
From mouth to mouth, there is she.
We have her.

In all her disgrace, there she is.
Her and me, together alone,
without finding each other or ourselves.
We have no way out, but still I sing.
She cries or gives in. It's all the same.

EL GRITÓN

He's here again in a dream,
our dead poet of Aztlán,
part pit bull, part santo,
a salt-and-pepper braid
crawling down his back,
the rings on his stubby fingers
(Taos silver and turquoise)
a faked Indianness.
He's improvising chants
on a napkin that doubles
for small-time bets.
We love the way he chafes
at the room in which he's trapped,
huaraches gummed to the carpet
where he stubs out a cigarette.
But when he starts to read
smoke coils around his head.
He quakes, yelps a name,
stricken by rising demons
that take up his dismal chords.
Bewildered now he stops,
pointing like the cold hand of a clock
at his silent open mouth
as rats flee from the pantry,
and behind them the wild, wild cats.

IN THE NAME OF THE GRANDFATHER

For Cipriano Rodríguez, 1887-1977

How many times shall I tell that old story?
How you were sired by a rich hacendado,
your mother a peasant girl poor as a flower,
how neither of them wanted you,
child of all we've become. Abandoned,
you fathered yourself, taking your name
from a man like you sweating out his life
in the pit of Salamanca, in the fields
that submerged you in their stalks of hell.
How you grew fast, married, and multiplied
your name, taking it north where your accent
rasped the ears of gringos who called you *boy*.

Who decided that you must search for work
to keep death behind like the world you left?
Who decreed your hard life in a tongue
strange to your nomadic Spanish?
In Texas, Iowa, Minnesota, Wyoming,
your children were your many hands
that cut and heaped the fruits of earth
whose unknown taste burned your tongue.
Then on a hilly colonia hugging the railyard
in Kansas City, you finally settled out
and became Papa Pano, a father
who arrived from the bottom of the world.

I never got to ask you what it was like.
Did America despise you or ignore you
or both? It always decided, even as your sons,
who knew only hunger and the demon of work,
went to war, returning to *dirty Mexican!*
in a land where deportation has been
the secret history of our life. But you never
muttered to yourself, en soledad, nor cursed
your corner of the world. You found
a vivid plot of earth, a tiny field of love
where grandchildren swelled la casita across the church
and memory ran longer than any night train.

More than the master's name or Indian's shame,
more than the family photos that curl in decay,
Rodríguez is scattered seeds and boxcars
passing between the breaths of lungs.
Rodríguez is a house of stars and dreams
whose generations leave their heat in me.
Rodríguez is a blessing upon my forehead
for the breaths and dreams and years to come.
I will tell that old story again and again,
I will pour it out full, beyond this now,
I will use it, for I'm a migrant too, alive
between two worlds where another, spreading, sings.

MALINCHE ON CORTÉS

I was happy to belong to him,
that goat with the black beard,
for he listened with respect
and heeded my counsel
when I became his tongue and guide.
The gift of speech was
my salvation. With him
I owned my desires,
not like with my people,
who gave me to strangers long ago
to glut a stepfather's wrath.
I hated them all but forgave
even my own mother,
who was wife before mother,
who trembled when I returned
with my Caxtillan tlaca,
my Castillian lord.
Calling me his queen,
he gave me precious stones
to give away. Yet I knew
he was an actor, helping
or hurting as the role demanded,
driven first and last by greed.
Then we entered the capitol.
Me, I too was dazzled by
all the gold, jade, and feathers.
See this ring? From Tenochtitlán.
O how swiftly the end came!
It's easy to remember.
He sat on the steps of skulls,
a new kind of priest, listening to
the city's fires murmur faintly.
That clarity of his mind,
that instinct for success
made me think he must be
terror's holiness
of Tiger, Snake, or Hawk.
What he was like at night

is the punishment in fullness
that still sings in my veins.
Martín.

I can see his face no more.
Only the ghost of touching
a dove in my arms appears.
He belongs to the one who left me
locked inside this hermitage,
above a smoky pestilential city
while he sailed home across
the waters of Anáhuac.
If I thought he would come back . . .
but the world belongs to his kind—
soldiers, users, inventors
of new words, who drive the nail home
when there's nothing more to win.
To him I am a shadow at most
in the features of his son,
but I am here. The dark woman.
Now the circle of silence
and dreams. I hear "love" spoken
in corners of this last place,
but who's speaking? My rapture
or his mockery?
O Mexicans!
Malinche tells you
that our lives move together
like a single wave.

RESEEDING THE CENTER

Walking beneath the trees
where wiggly shadows

work toward us
I feel we're inside

body's light
hot and seared with veins

Your swishing skirt
stirs voices in the dust

and I hear the name
of the city in the lake

darkening the air
with its Om

We're no longer in the sphere of day
but standing nightwatch

by the waters of Anáhuac
the surf gently hissing

the Star Hunter slowly
dipping into the black of sea-sky

Then my familiar dream-shape
emerges at the rim

and lifts its head
from that indigo world

to speak of green dawns
painted with snails

and the book of days
that rules dreams and hearts

I lean into its scales
that spark reflections there

tablelands a white city
sun-steps rising over rooftops

I climb stone over stone
rising into another man

the flute I hear behind me
your voice singing

You're here remember this
as I reach the top

earth, sky, and song
a veil tearing off into the wind.

THE KISS

You said my kiss was like rain
chipping at the window,
and felt tingling in the bones,
incandescent, marrow deep.

Your kiss is like the memory
of night fluttering at the pane,
where eyes as old as sea stones
watch us curl into a flower.

The light of those huge eyes
strikes a black world here—
wild roads, streams of skin,
gossamer oozings, flames
in the thin nighttime shower.

How you sway in the shadows,
and that taste on my tongue
that burns, that taste of us . . .
The air turns red, and a rainy night
rolls over us with dripping wings.

SINCE HE WAS A BOY

Joaquin has had long hair since he was a boy.
His mother kept it shiny black with beer and a cold rinse.
Tonight, he tells me, that it's only been short once.
He was nine and all his brothers and sisters got lice.
Joaquin remembers the long thick braid of his hair
on the bathroom floor, swept away and thrown into the trash.
Joaquin tells me that later that night he
dug through the garbage to find his braid,
but it was lost beneath opened cans of
dog food, vegetable peelings, and chicken bones.
Joaquin's eyes are like a river when he tells me this.
Beside me on the bed, he knows I'm jealous.
I tell him that today my blow dryer got so hot, it turned itself off.
I went to work with wet hair.
This is when Joaquin releases his hair from the ponytail,
leans over me,
and lets his hair spill against my skin so I know better
the little boy
who has retrieved what he lost.

KOOTIES

I can still feel the gust of air
from the quick turn of one pig-tailed girl
to another
informing each other
that a kiss from a boy could cause "kooties."
In the third grade, after recess, Jerome Ortiz gave me kooties.
All the girls teased until hushed by Mrs. Casey
who asked, "what are kooties?"
I explained to her that I hadn't felt the effects of kooties yet,
but feared they would take me over in the dark as I slept.
"Are they monsters?" she asked and I became the teacher.
I told her kooties were much worse than monsters
and even La Llorona.
My mother said I talked crazy and
explained that kooties only existed on fountain spouts
or from kissing little doggies,
but not from little boys and certainly not from Jerome Ortiz;
he came from a good family.
I listened and tried to repeat my mother's wise words
          to my classmates,
but they encircled me in shame and sang "you've got kooties!"

In the third grade my reputation for kooties stuck with me.
And at the age of 15, my kooties became a baby boy
with dark curly hair and green eyes.
I named him Jerome, after the boy who kissed me
on a double dare, ruined my life,
and never knew that I loved him.

BREAKING PIÑATAS

Help me understand what's happening to our families
our little brothers are locked up in penitentiaries
our little sisters are being treated like mistresses,
I'm sick of this
it's getting ridiculous
let's put an end to this

mass abomination against the Children of Aztlán
we're People of the Sun but now the targeted ones
Congress the government recruiting from the ignorant
to be puppets of intimidation spreading misinformation

promoting fear and hate, so why do we tolerate
acts of injustice discrimination and bigotry
prepárense mi gente,
or fall victims to this conspiracy

Racial retaliation cultural annihilation,
family separation community devastation
broken promises of freedom and liberty
food on the table and a roof for your families

all you have to do is work for nickels and dimes
and when gas prices get higher put your sons' lives on the line
but we've worked for next to nothing did it with honor and pride
and when America called our sons went off to war and died

served with nobility praying for the possibility
that we'd be accepted as citizens not treated with hostility
World War II, Korea, and Vietnam
Desert Storm and even in Afghanistan
blood has spilled how soon you forget
what about the many rivers of tears that they've wept?

but still they have dreams in shades of Red White and Blue
everything they have they want to share with you
two eagles sharing one serpent two flags sharing one wind
two neighbors sharing two cultures
two children playing on the same land

BROWN EYES IN BLUES

I place this badge on my chest
Tuck a cross in my bulletproof vest
Say a quick prayer before checking my shoes—
Perfectly shined, of course—and well-pressed blues

I hesitate before looking in the mirror
That's when visions of Malinche appear
Because nothing really looks out of place
Until I see the brown skin of my own face

Malinche talks to me. Her voice, soft as Mother's, chimes
"Don't worry hombre you look just fine
Don't worry what people say that's beyond your control"
Then why is my heart waging war with my soul?

Brown eyes in blues what's wrong with this picture?
My job is my love though my soul screams "How could you?"
Why can't I be appreciated for all I'm giving?
Why am I so proud to get shot at and spit on for a living?

When I wear the badge as I stroll through the barrio
Malinche walks beside me "Don't worry mijo I'll guide you"
On the other side the spirits of those that came before me
Cuahtémoc Zapata Chávez have paid the price for me

"Malinche is right" they say
"You have to march on with this burden
It doesn't really matter if they
understand you wear this badge for them"

A cop at your service Chicano with a gun
A product of two immigrants the barrio's son
I bleed for the weak sometimes cry for the young
I'm the angel sent for the children of no one

When duty calls I protect and serve
The good the bad even those you think don't deserve
I wear the badge with honor and pride

While my soul keeps reminding me who I am inside

Every now and then I drop to my knees and beg for mercy
As my heart mind and soul take a beating it hurts me!!

I look in the mirror one more time
Now Jesus is holding Malinche's hand and mine

I take a deep breath before I start my patrol
For a moment there's peace between heart and soul
The barrio calls for me I can't refuse
'Cause I know they'll be safe with brown eyes in blues

ES MÍO

Some things are easily stolen while other things are hard to take

Some things are easily broken while other things are impossible to break

My mind my soul my dignity my culture and my pride

are things that you can't take or break no matter how hard you may try

You see my gente have paid for the things I have with rivers of blood sweat and tears

But still today you try to take away as you have been for 500 years

Chico Méndez spoke Ruben Salazar wrote Cesar Chávez marched in peace

Villa rebelled Hidalgo yelled Zapata refused to live on his knees

All have passed on their spirits I carry on remembering them every-time I wake

Cuauhtémoc's spirit will guide me so go ahead and try me I promise you I will not break

MUJER DE MI VIDA

for Rose Sepulveda

My life has been filled with many riches but the most important is your
Unconditional love you've laughed with me cried for me cared for me
Just like an angel from above
Every time I've fallen you were there to break the fall I'd
Run from you and disappointed you often, but that
Didn't seem to matter to you at all and
Even when I'd run away, you'd pray that I'd be all right and when
My father left us it was you who taught me how to fight
I've become a respected man and it is you who I give my thanks to you taught me the
Values of life so I thank you for being a great father too
I don't know how you did it but a strong woman you definitely are you
Didn't finish school, and still you've pushed me far. One day I will marry
And maybe have a son and if he should ever need a role model
MUJER DE MI VIDA you raised the perfect one GRACIAS MAMÁ.

BUÑUELOS

here I stand en la cocina
trying to recapture those times
when during New Year's Eve
mamá used to make me buñuelos

here I stand, in a white man's kitchen,
neighborhood, town, state and country
a thousand miles from my South Texas

far from the barrio
where the neighbors congregate
to bid el Año Viejo farewell

conjunto music blarring, accordion
guitars and guapangos
kids shooting off illegal fireworks
running to hide behind car tires
when the police drove past

run, run, the chota is coming!
I don't know what gave us
more of a rush, hiding from the police
or watching the bottle-rockets
near miss the neighbor's rooftop

far from el barrio where everyone
starts celebrating temprano
bailes at El Villareal and
El Centro Cívico

daddy firing his
32 revolver at midnight

I remember eating
leftover tamales from Christmas
capirotada
with lots of peanuts and
queso amarillo

NO, I am instead
frying lop-sided and chewy
buñuelos in Ottawa, Kansas
Wondering why—I didn't pay more attention
Wondering why—I can't remember her recipe

buñuelos: fried dough, covered with cinnamon & sugar
cocina: kitchen
barrio: neighborhood
el Año Viejo: old year
conjuntos/guapangos: music bands/style of dance
chota: policeman
temprano: early
bailes: dances
El Centro Cívico: Civic Center
capirotada: Mex. bread pudding
queso amarillo: yellow cheese (cheddar)

next to the Car Wash
at the Snow Wiz
is where I would buy
raspas de coco
tamarindo y limón
a pitcher full
for about two dollars
25 cents extra
and you could get
the sweet cream topping

hacienda cola
watching the cholos
bathe their hydraulic women
with abuelita's quarters
too "chulo" to get a job

el Valle
hell on the tip of Texas
sucking on bolis de fresa
water balloon fights
para los huercos
drinking Joyas
afuera en el porche
to wash down
the boiled shrimp
mamá prepared
with her special sauce
mustard y ketchup

el caliche mirage
flowing por las calles
del barrio
río chico río negro
sweet warmth
soft on my toes
but black
as the hair on them

raspas de coco: coconut snow cones
tamarindo y limón: tamarind & lime
hacienda cola: queueing
cholos: Chicano gang members
abuelita: grandmother
chulo: good-looking
el Valle: Rio Grande Valley (South TX)
bolis de fresa: Mexican Flavor Ice (strawberry flavor)
para los huercos: for the rugrats
Joya: Mexican soda brand
afuera en el porche: outside on the porch
el caliche mirage: tar mirage
por las calles: thru the streets
del barrio: of the neighborhood

EL NEGRITO

I lived on Evans St.
La Pulga, the local flea market,
was along the railroad tracks.
It blocked my barrio from the *other side*.
I rarely crossed the tracks unless
I was walking over to visit my best friend Janice.
La Bolilla, as my parents referred to her.
She was taller than all of the boys in 6th grade.
Strands of hair the color of fideo framed
her freckled face.
"What if they touched?" I often wondered.
"Would they form into small patches the color of my caramelo skin?"
Janice lived on the *other side* and she never shopped at La Pulga.

The *other side*, on the south side of the tracks,
they had parks with picnic tables that weren't
chained to cement cinder blocks, automatic garage doors,
indoor pets, pension plans and central air.
Who in the barrio needed central air anyway?
Take my house, for example,
we had four window air conditioning units
in a five-room house.
So what if the breakers blew?
That was just another excuse
to take off an extra item of clothing.
Air conditioners were what brought us people from our barrio together.
Since the windows were always corked with those buzzing
electricity hogs, you couldn't spy on your neighbors.
So we met and talked with our neighbors, cara a cara.

But, even with the air conditioning units on a high setting,
the commotion of the Pulga drew you in.
El Negrito used to wake me every second Sunday morning
of the month. He preached at La Pulga.
You could hear el Negrito's voice pleading,
repentance resonating from his speakers.
He would sing hymns to the angels that drew you to pay
the one quarter fee it took to get through the entrance gate.

Once inside, you would be drawn to his stage, a patch of earth,
where he scattered the dirt and spit into his microphone,
Hallelujah ...the Devil... knock'n ...at my door...
but I.. turn to Jesus and he sav'n my soul ... praise Jesus...
keep a knock'n... but my soul be saved!
His tootsie rolled grin and choreographed wrinkles—
doubting your salvation.

El Negrito, the traveling preacher could be found
by the booth that sold shoes. It couldn't get any better;
you could buy plastic huaraches and
get saved by Jesus all in one trip.
He was to me the bearded woman at the circus.
He was to me the penitentes I once witnessed
at San Juan de los Lagos, heading to the Basílica on their knees,
bloodied by the cobble stones they crawled on.

I had never before seen a negrito. I had seen a picture
of one in the Lotería we played on the weekends.
This negrito didn't wear yellow slacks, a turquoise
suit jacket or a pair of black and white wing tipped shoes
like the one in Lotería.
He didn't wear a straw hat with a red band
with matching bow tie and red flower on his suit jacket.
And, he didn't smile white.

El Negrito: black man
La Pulga: flea market
barrio: neighborhood
La Bolilla: derogatory for "white girl"
fideo: Mexican spaghetti
caramelo: caramel
cara a cara: face to face
huaraches: sandals
penitentes: penitents
basílica: shrine
Lotería: Mex. bingo

KANSAS

I know when they harvest winter wheat,
when corn needs to be planted, and how
close to God people think they are.
But I don't know one multi-tongued latino,
where I can buy pumpkin empanadas,
dulce de leche and De La Rosa Mazapán.
Whether La Llorona roams in white or black
in these parts and what creeks she frequents.
I cannot remember how
a wetback smells anymore,
soon after he crosses el Río Grande—
the vein of my roots meandering
in hues of azul.

empanadas: pies
dulce de leche: caramel
mazapan: peanut butter candy
La Llorona: the legendary wailing woman
(Mexican Tale)
azul: blue

LA OSCURIDAD

secret reading
flashlight
candle
libros cómicos
Periquita
Memín
y La Pequeña Lulú

bed
blinds venetian
picket fence
cracks
coal light
glow-
in-the dark-
rosary

teddy bear
doll
faces
babbling
mid-
nite

pillows
three
east barrio
north
west
suffocating
cotton face

feet
blanket
embrace
may the devil
not
lick my toes

LA REINA OF CHOCOLATE COVERED CHERRIES

times   many
i made you cry
because
i wouldn't learn
to make
tortillas

womanhood
measured
by number of times
you
burn
your fingertips
on the comal

La Reina: the queen
comal: round earthenware griddle

LA TRENZA

as we sat
together
you grooming
my hair
i felt
a painful tug
(the brush
had met a knot)
"¡Sanaviche!"
i screamed

the following
morning
you brushed
braided
my hair
took me to
the Salón de Belleza
where a pair
of scissors
taught me
your lesson

mamá a machete
would have been
more appropriate

seven years
past
i found my trenza
neatly wrapped
in plastic

i asked
why
you kept it
you told me

"para recordar
el día que el Diablo
se te metió"

trenza: braid
Sanaviche: son of a bitch
Salón de Belleza: beauty salon
para recordar el día que el Diablo se te metio:
to remember the day that the Devil
possessed you

LA PULGA

Tía Julia and Tío Antonio had a booth at La Pulga.
You could buy almost anything there, Pedro Infante
8-track tapes, rusty tools, avocados,
wash tubs from Mexico and talismans that you could
use to put a curse on your ex-lover. There was even
a booth that sold Avon beauty products. There
you could smell rancid lipstick and honeysuckle from
the Sweet Honesty body splash.

I always stopped by my tíos' booth
to say hello, give them a beso and an abrazo,
pick up the toston that was always waiting for me,
a shiny fifty cent piece of silver.
"Ten mija, comprate una raspa o una soda,"
Tía Julia would say.

They loved children.
Tía Julia and Tío Antonio lived on Egly, one street over and
one block east from Evans Street (where I lived)
I used to visit them during the summer school
vacation because their household was
restless and captivating. The outdoor of their house
was like a tropical jungle. They had exotic birds,
parrots and parakeets hung in outdoor cages.
The parrots whistled at you and ranted, "I'm so chulo!"
"Mami wants a beso!" "¡¡Cotorro, Cotorrito!!" (whistle)
The tíos also had cats, dogs, rabbits
and chickens. Their house was like a petting zoo,
but they didn't breed iguanas or anything like that,
they bred children instead. I could always count on one
of their nine children being home to entertain me.

I also enjoyed Tía Julia's stories.
She always had a thoughtful story about
her sister-in-law, my biological mother, who had
given me up for adoption when I was several days old.
Tía Julia somehow felt that she needed to
apologize to me for being born from the groin

of that mujer, "We wanted you mija, but we couldn't
even feed our own children," is what I often heard from the
many uncles and aunts. "It's okay Tía," I would assure her,
"Daddy y mi mamá provide me all that I need. Besides, I like
being an only child."

And on my return back home, I'd rub
the fifty cent John F. Kennedy that I'd dropped into
my pant pocket.
Knowing that—I didn't have to share it with anyone.

La Pulga: flea market
tío/tía: uncle/aunt
abrazo/beso: hug and kiss
mija: slang for my daughter (endearment)
Ten mija, comprate una raspa o una soda:
buy yourself a snow cone or a soda
chulo: good looking
Mami wants a beso: mama wants a kiss
mujer: woman

MY ORIGINAL SIN

I found a single red rose petal in a book
purchased at the Dusty Bookshelf,
Loose Woman, by Sandra Cisneros.
The lone petal marked a poem entitled— "Original Sin."
The one that says—

... without original
sin ... like the good
girl ...

Sandra the good girl,
would have never shared with anyone this story
of a seduction. Seduced by the stranger in the hallway,
the one that smiled, made an extra effort to make eye contact.
"I've been admiring you from afar," he'd said
"I can't help myself, with your permission, may I touch you?"
"May I run my fingers through your hair?"
Get them caught, giving him an excuse to embrace you.

Sandra the good girl, would have never kissed warm, silky lips,
suave, like the foreskin of pipí...and liked it.
They never would have chuckled when at the housing projects
the ones across from Whataburger
and the city pool, she lost her virginity.

Good girls would not have told about that white towel
the boy had placed underneath.
The terry cloth that was to catch the drops of crimson,
threads of hymen flesh.
"Okay, I am ready," she would say nervously.
Approaching her,
she'd chuckle at the sight of him in his underwear.

What of the power she thought she'd feel,
going from señorita to mujer.
As he knelt and laid over her, the smell of
his cologne—Avon's Wagon Wheel,
dripping from his armpits.

He was the pace of corn tortillas,
masa de maize pounded by the palm of hands.
Reshaping the curvature
of the hips, she'd reject his bloodline.

When it was all over, he drove her home.
She cried in the shower that night.
Thankful, her father hadn't noticed
that she was wearing her blouse inside out.
She cried in the shower that night,
from too much laughter
—her man wore red bikini underwear.

suave: smooth
pipi: penis
señorita: young girl
mujer: woman
masa de maize: corn tortilla dough

SIN CALZÓN

I want to roam
the streets at night
pantiless
loose
when only the sidewalk
watches
stay up all night
read your diary
broadcast your secrets
on the 10 o'clock news

memoir
of a serial bore
you kill me
with your consonants
the way those *r*'s
roll off your tongue
like leather
in those shoes
at the foot of your bed

Out of spite
I place a bag
of Stayfree maxi pads
in your bathroom cabinet
signaling
to other women
that you are taken

I want to
come and go
as I please
hand me your one
spare key
I'll add it
to my collection

UNDER THE EARTH

Under the earth, frente del porche
Under the tree which breeds furry
gusanitos that squirt
Moco green when you step on them

I hid rubies, caniconas and cats eyes
Treasures of my childhood
If you dig in the backyard,
Fleabite's set of teeth,
The dog that was muy sentida
Cried when you scolded her

Also, a doll that someone buried,
Sin cabeza, a product of witchcraft
My mother would say
It was probably las Tías
Who hate mamá because
She is from another land
El otro lado, they say
A place where there are no treasures
A wasteland

But I know that they are wrong
For I remember the hollow echo
Of my footsteps
Under the cherimoya tree
On the land where mamá was born
She tells me that it's buried treasure
As she shows me the Spanish gold coins
She once unearthed

frente del porche: in front of the porch
gusanitos: worms
moco: booger
caniconas: shooter marbles
muy sentida: very sensitive
sin cabeza: headless
las Tías: the aunts
el otro lado: the other side (Mexico)
cherimoya: fruit, where flavor is suggestive of the pineapple and banana

CORRIDO: MINING TOWN BLUES
(Sing and Don't Cry Beautiful Brown-Skin Girl)

The cassette player turns,
Low strumming guitars stream out
toward the ceiling
off the walls—louder still.
Violins fill the room with Spanish
rancheros and corridos.

I bask in the beat
the words spoon out of my lips.
My tongue forks to form the
rolling sounds of the Spanish words.
As Linda Ronstadt sings, the sound
penetrates every pore of my brown skin.

"She is like the lark that builds its nest among the
strongest of branches ... and others are like the
deer, killed unexpectedly while looking for love ..."

My brother still sings these songs
with free abandon
the same songs that blast
out of the radio
out of the stereo,
out of his high-pitched voice—
the pain of serenade to an unseen lover:

My brother danced corridos with
an ever so slight move of the hips,
moving from left to right,
shuffling across the dance floor,
side by side—corrido cool—
the boy who loved the girl
with green eyes.

28 girls loved my brother—
the suave dancer who could
sway the cool sway to corridos,
the same corridos he sings to the

green eyes of his heart.
"Beautiful green-eyed girl,
what am I to do when you take
this love away from me?"

Heart broken, he jitterbugged
summers away with me—the best dancers
to the peppermint twist—to corridos
And at mamá's wake, his tenor rang
out in harmony ... "*Ay ... ay ... ay ... ay ...*
canta y no llores, porque cantando
se alegran cielito lindo los corazónes. . ."

My earliest memory is of mamá crooning
this song outside the adobe while she stirred a
boiling black pot full of clothes, steam rising
above her head, and I, blissfully under a
stand of trees in a place where the sun did not
interrupt watching the birds land safely on the
branches above while mamá sang her song:

"Ay *... ay ... ay ... ay ... canta y no llores ...*"

Words to these songs sit stored on the shelf
of my mind; the Spanish words emerge
sometimes in the middle of a conversation.
The flawed "*Sh*" sound forming off my tongue.

The day we left our adobe behind,
the brown face of my brother
towered above me as we held unto the
splintered railing of the green pick-up—
his voice crooning with the
clanking rhythm of the truck—
On tiptoes we stared as the dust
billowed up from around the sides,
catching our faces
pellets stinging our cheeks for
100 miles as we
went to find our wood house—

A wood house sat on cement
stilts, smelter ruins that became

Our playground where we
played each night until dark, making
up games we dared not tell about
in that endless desert of blue
mining town blue
wood house blue
where papá drove the dynamite

Truck around that big open-pit,
where trickles of water
found its way out of
the big hole
the open-pit mine hole
the company hole where
water crept out from

Mine shafts, down cliffs,
through cracks
forming puddles of
turquoise blue—
the constant washing of copper ore
scouring the ground bare

A town built on top of ghost towns,
sons still sweat the brow of
their fathers and fathers before—
cheap labor of the Southwest where
Chinamen, Irishmen and Mexicans
all sucked the mountain clean—

Hungry and eager, they laid their mats
on the rich iron ore and found no escape,
no escape from the endless desert where the sun
beats hot on twisted cacti—

where orange and yellow poppies
pop out of the ground tracking in the colors
that fill the crooked shapes.

"Ay ... ay ... ay ... canta y no llores"
"Sing and don't cry, beautiful brown-skin girl."

LOVE AND MADNESS TAKE ON MANY FORMS I FIND

I. Circles

A well
sinking
running love
I play like a fool
in the water
writing circles all
over me
not touching

A well
sinking
staying
running deeper
writing circles all over me
not touching

A well
sinking
staying
playing like a fool—
a deep pool
writing circles all over me
not touching

II. And I go on eating ice cream

Captive for a
year-and-a-half
I go on eating
ice-cream

The widow
cleverly disguised in white
lured its prey

Her weaving
bound my feet between
silken threads—

My ice-cream is homemade

III. Ribbons for my hair

I only wanted
ribbons for my
hair but
he played
old songs and
showed me
pictures without faces

Every morning the
ancient God
drew pictures on
the chalked wall of
my room—telling
stories of rainstorms
and his glory of youth—

I dreamed of
pretty shoes and
ribbons for my hair.
One night in my dream
my imaginary cat
talked to me and said

"He just lives off
other peoples' money"—
I saw myself shoot him
twice but still he did not
hear what I had to say.

IV. The Box

My box is
found—
let it remain
unopened
the contents are mine
misshapen—
let Pandora open it
.

MASA TEARS

There are times
when everyone's gone
I lie on my bed and wait
I go back to the

brown dust and dirt
from the sperm my Padre
emptied into my
Madre's womb—

to the aliveness that
spills on the
damask cover—and
I live inside a big

white-washed house—
the one where my
Tio Manford was caretaker—
the mayordomo's house

through pink curtains I
see a field of green grass
flowers not real in
desert land—I see

a tall black iron
fence and brown children
caked in dirt playing
in the hot sun—

the fence won't let them
come into the garden
Awake my eyes drape bare
dripping pellets thick as Mama's
tortillas—masa tears

WALLED MOUNTAIN GHOST TOWN

Morenci Morenci where have you gone
under the ground and beyond?
What is left of you strange city you were just a
town built on top of ghost towns covered
over and over again by iron-machines
memories too old and dry to be resurrected but
memories still that will not go away
how did you leave such an imprint if all the
houses and hills and PD stores are buried deep
in that hole that continues to get deeper?

Is it that so many souls were born to live there,
walled mountain town for a short time be schooled so
intensely in the school of life making us who we are,
resilient remembering who we were and why we were
lumped together learned together more soldiers from
one place dying together for a country they knew
so little about? All that made survival a promise for
even the timid—how you molded our minds and wills
and desire to leave you as fast as we could but not
forget you even after 40 years

Morenci Morenci that place of yearning for what?
We only knew of the poverty and the hunger that
brought us all into your enveloping prison walls—
hardened-earth walls laden streaked with iron ore
a seducing temptress holding even those who invented
you in its grasp PD owned us then and owns a part of us
still It wasn't enough for you to let us live in shacks,
the worst for those with names like López Martinez and
Peña—the Smiths and Jones and Williams lived in places
with names like Plansite and Stargo Hill
(We hiked up and down dirt trails and made rusted
smelter ruins our playground)

Out of you came us—would-be poets inspired
only by those who came and stayed when they didn't
have to; you seduced them too Morenci—they gave with

passion and we survived and drew our strength from
their books and their staying and their excitement to
make us learn and listen to all the battles of the civil war
when they didn't know we were living our own civil war in the
'60s when Chicanos congregated on one side of Morenci
high school and whites on the other—and when the votes
came in for homecoming king and queen—the only power
brown knew was to vote in numbers

Morenci Morenci how you twisted your company upon us
owning our homes the stores all our money going back to
your Fortune 500 Company and finally wrenched your PD
arm on the $12 an hour jobs in '83—the sweat of our fathers
and brothers drenched out of them under that Arizona sun
when copper wasn't selling so good—while PD sat in cool
New York offices with their New York lawyers deciding fate
to an already raped people You didn't flinch to send an
armament of tanks National Guard and helicopters to break
their strike Your power left its mark in 1917 and again in
1983—you win again PD You always do

But Bobby Andozola stood for all those fathers and brothers
whose sweat you had drenched He stood in the scorch of
black asphalt in the middle of Highway 66 with arms
outstretched in the form of a martyr's cross—and we
heard—2,000 miles away we heard—24 years later we still
hear the words he yelled over your mountain and we
understand his plea—

"In the name of the Lord God" he yelled out "would you do
this to your own brothers and sisters?"

Then the tear-gas flew out and Bobby Andozola's shoes
came off—then his shirt came off and his pants he flung
toward them too—with sleight of hand you strip your people
PD, as easy as you strip the earth—layer by layer—
with iron and claw down to the bare bone leaving only
ghosts

MY UNCLE, AGE 93, IS ARRESTED AND DETAINED SIX HOURS FOR BLOCKING THE ENTRANCE TO THE U.S. NAVAL BASE IN VIEQUES, PUERTO RICO, AFTER A LIVE BOMB KILLS AND INJURES CIVILIANS

—for Carlos Vélez-Rieckehoff

"Born that way," his mother, my grandmother, would say,
in the same tone she would use to explain genius
or Siamese twins. At sixteen Carlos took off
with the Stars and Stripes from the Capitol and hid
in the hills, where the guardia civil never found him-
who would betray him, their hero, doing what they
lacked the courage to do? In the fifties he flew
the outlawed flag of his country on the roof of
his farmhouse where all the villagers could see it
and revel in the illusion that they were free.
The judge offered him leniency if he'd recant.
¡Soy nacionalista hasta los cojones!-
they claim he cried (he claims they lied). He spent the next
three years in "La Princesa," a euphemism
for the San Juan federal penitentiary,
much of the time in solitary confinement.
Yesterday Don Carlos, tall and elegant in
his white suit, the sea breezes ruffling his white hair,
trekked the miles across Vieques on his walker, up
the Sisyphean hill, for his final act of
defiance. "Good," I tell my mother, "he'll assume
he's still a threat to colonialism. Now he
can die with pride." It's comforting to think one has
power in one's old age. Four years ago, during
a hurricane that devastated Borinquen,
my husband asked his friend, a retired admiral,
to check on Carlos, see if he had survived.
When the Navy knocked at his door, Carlos was sure
they had come to arrest him, though he'd done nothing.
"Can't blame him," my mother says. "Why should he trust them?"
Today he stands with Robert Kennedy, Jr.,
and other dignitaries from the States, and waits

for the gavel to sentence him this one last time.

Gardia civil: Civil Guard
La Princesa: The Princess
Soy nacionalista hasta los cojones: I'm a Nationalist down to my balls
Borinquen: Indian name for Puerto Rico, the oldest colony in the world

BY THE DAWN'S EARLY LIGHT

Three Kings Day, 1991

I can't sleep thinking about the men and
women—children, really—buried out there
in those endless waves of sand, fear
and fire grabbing at their ankles, sweat
keeping custody of their souls,
their St. Jude's face-down in the dunes.
I can't sleep thinking about them
lost out there, naked in their trust. Maybe
they're dreaming of amber waves
back home, the cold light of a Kansas
morning, when they'd dawdle in bed,
bracing themselves for the chores
they'd have to tend before walking
the dark roads to school, hands aching
from the pull and squeeze of milking cows,
shoulders stiff and sore from the scrape
of the shovel against the barn floor,
manure slapping it with a wet thud.
I read how they have to sleep in shifts—
"hot sheets" we used to call it—all housed
in the same barn-like barracks, the women
having to dress under the blankets,
to ward off the groping eyes and hands
of men who may one day save them
from the eyes and hands of other men.

It was so cold here last night
the weatherman, a jolly grey-suited
Santa with a wand, told us we wouldn't
want to *know* the wind/chill factor,
but his wand raised the temperature
for tomorrow and the next day and
a happy little sun-faced god appeared
on the bottom left corner of the screen
to signal hope for the freezing Midwest.

Outside, the umber twigs and trunks

of shadowless trees look haphazard,
as though dumped there by a lumberjack

in a hurry or blown up by a hand grenade,
some sticking upright in the snow,
others frozen in space like a 2-D
nightmare Currier & Ives might
have been trying to forget, or redefine.

The one car in the distance still
has its lights on as it heads
toward the one star in the east.

On a branch of a nearby tree, one fixed
red ball hangs on like a Christmas ornament
someone forgot to put away. Something
long like a ribbon of blood flickers
once then twice the way our arms and legs
twitch in our sleep. Have I caught
this cardinal dreaming his taped dream?
Is the eagle swooping down on him again?
Or is he getting a signal from some far off
place that *this* is the day, and, like
the rest of us, he has a long trek ahead?

KNIFE

She was old. She lived alone in a small house
two blocks away. When they found her, days after,
she had been stabbed seventeen times—as if
a host of assassins had struck an empress down.
She might even have looked up briefly
before the final cut, spurting blood and
an imperious last line or two. Perhaps not.
Perhaps the first wound had done the trick—
the rest sport for the mad or wicked. A handyman
lived nearby. He worked odd jobs while leading
a secret life with his neighbor's Anglo wife,
who would sneak him in when her husband
and her son were out. No one questioned
Sanchez about the old lady. He traveled alone.
This was a gang job. One day while walking past
a vacant lot close by the boy spots a shiny
object winking at him through layers of rust
like a cheap sequin—summoning him to stoop
down, swoop it up, later to brandish it
with pride before his mother's sucked
astonishment. Give it here, she says.
The name on the crudely carved handle is clear,
letters printed in black Magic Marker—but
are they clearly the handyman's? Sanchez
is a common name. She knows he doesn't stand
a chance if he stands trial. Knows they'll find
guilt hidden like stacks of money unexplained
beneath the floorboards of his mind. She knows
Texas. Knows how stuff gets planted when you're
a Mexican without an alibi and they need
a solution. And most of all she knows, knows
as she digs the tiny grave for the homemade knife,
knows as she pats the soil over it and sows
the seeds of justice, knows as she pours
a 50-50 mixture of water and fish emulsion
over it to make the seeds grow, knows, damn it,
she just knows that he is guilty as hell.

LYDIA'S PHANTASMAGORIA

And tonight's headline news:
All of Puerto Rico watches as TV's Queen of Soaps
is condemned to life imprisonment. Stay tuned.

High,
like when you're in a glass elevator going up
and you feel stationary
and everything around you seems to be going down,
dropping,
slipping slowly away:
the light switch slinking down the wall, the vase
full of flowers sinking beneath the painting
over the mantel, the Ralph Goings painting of a woman—
could be any woman, though he calls her Shanna,
sitting at a Kentucky Fried Chicken window booth—
a woman left suddenly, left alone,
left incomplete as though half of her had fallen
away, disappeared out of sight,
the two cups of coffee on the table unsipped,
growing clotted and cool like the relationship,
the cigarette between her fingers
no longer sparkling, but smouldering imperceptibly
like the one who left, is left,
and the cross-legged woman left behind reworks,
rephrases the parting words,
restructures, relives the final scene,
repossesses what may or may not have been said (she
can't remember), so that it hurts less,
maybe even comes out right
with a musical comedy ending of forever
and ever amen and all that crap and caramba.
But it's not that way—not that time,
not this time, not then, not now, not ever, and
the word that can heal gets mislaid, misfired,
feelings misstated, misconstrued,
justice miscarried, sometimes all the way to the chair,
and not the one looking out from
Colonel Sanders' place—that's art, that's fiction,
this is life, death. This is murder.

In the beginning. . . hell, there is no beginning,
only a question and answer period to start
and the questions are loaded and the answers are invariably
wrong
and these two, like the couple in the Goings painting,
they tried—we all try.
The story goes (and I have no reason to doubt it)
that Lydia did him in—
that one night while making love—a long time coming round,
too long—Luis made the fatal slip, calling her
by the other one's name.
Had she still been in the throes of ecstasy
his Nydia might have sneaked by undetected,
but as patience would have it, she heard,
stiffened beneath him,
her body hard and flat and dry;
his, finally spent, sprawling like a lead sheet
across the glass bones of her rage—and
in that moment
she knew he had deceived her
and knowing,
waited,
waited until the time was right,
playing at the game of love while playing for time,
not yet knowing what to do
but knowing something had to be done, someone
done in.
She plotted in the only way she knew—Dantesquely
fitting the punishment to the crime.
She hired three (already a mistake, a stupid mistake,
3 x 2 = 6 too many
involved, too many palms to grease,
bucks to pass) thugs, hired three thugs to kill him.
But first the slow revenge—intense,
steady—because death after all is liberation,
slow revenge is pain: an imprisonment of self
within self, a double jeopardy of torture.
Satisfied, she rubbed her hands with wicked glee
and laughed *¡Ja! ¡Ja!* adding

the Spanish equivalent of "you bastard, you'll moan
and groan for *me* before I'm through!" (Hijo de la gran. . . etcetera.)

On January 6th the three thugs—kings for a day—
kidnapped him and delivered him blindfolded
to a nondescript, out-of-the-way room
in a bourgeois suburb of San Juan
that smelled of chorizos and habichuelas.
Miramar without a view—no ocean, no sky, no moon, no place
for the reigning stars of Puerto Rican soaps to be caught dead in.
And, waiting for him, his patient wife—
legs crossed, cigarette smouldering like the one
in the painting—eye ready behind
an instantaneously gratifying
Kodakcolorpolaroid,
its protruding flashbulb palpitating
like a stud in heat—ready to document the brilliant defeat
of Luis in particular, man in general, ready to
show him falling from dignity,
from hope, from grace,
from the top of the popularity polls (*click!*)
falling (*click!*) to ignominy and low, low ratings.
And she ascending on that elevator
getting high, higher,
snapping and flashing
picture (*click!*) after picture
of his long, slow descent.

He might have stepped backwards out of an open window
on the 31st floor of the C.B.S. building
and fallen to his death in 5 and 9/10ths of a second,
but instead he was snapped up,
snapped over and over again, his wounds hissing
in vivid color,
his tiny parts removed one by one—
a nail (*click!*), an earlobe (*click!*),
a testicle (*click! click! click! click! click!*)—missing
except in the snapshots strewn face up
across the blood-soaked bittersweet shag carpet.
And Luis missing the good lines,

missing the applause—
Oh baby missing you-oo-oo-oo, oh baby missing you-hooo-oo—
missing all but the last laugh—
between socorros (Pietá never had it so good)
he damned her and cursed her and spited her
with cries for Nydia! Nydia! Nydia!
which sounded to her like the *nya-nya-nyaaaah*
of vengeful siblings,
and suddenly Lydia felt his anguish, his anger.
Saw his hatred.
And to shut out a reflection of her own loathsomeness,
she ordered the three assassins
to pluck out his eyes (*click! click!*).
Nearly out of film she had them stuff his body
into his car, douse it with gasoline,
set it on fire. Strains of aguinaldos drifted in
through the open window—abrir la puerta al niño
que está pidiendo amparo. . . etcetera.

Steadying the camera on the second-storey window ledge,
the craggy bricks carving deep ridges into her elbows,
she snaps the final spectacle from above.
And Lydia becomes the flames—
teasing, playful, at first—her fingers
combing the fringes of the orange floral bedspread,
pulling off each petal—
he loves me, he loves me not—
unfolding each leaf, each bud, her tongue
reading his skin like Braille—every pore,
every mole, every tangled curl telling a different story,
spelling a new name—
he loves her, he loves me not.
As the flames rise
higher and higher past her window
she tilts the camera up toward the soiled sky,
and all at once she feels herself sinking
irreversibly
as though she were on an elevator
plummeting
through the earth's mantel,

deep, deep into the magma of memory,
beyond hope, beyond redemption, beyond *revision*,
watching everything,
everything she had ever wanted,
everything she had ever loved, evanesce—
watching her whole life
go up in smoke.

Trailer: *Tune in next week to the first episode
of* Love and Murder: On Screen and Off, *featuring
that hot new sensation Nydia Estrella,
in the title role of* Lydia (click! click! click!).

socorros: cries for help
habichuelas: beans
aguinaldos: Christmas carols
abrir la puerta al niño que está pidiendo amparo:
open the door to the child begging for shelter

new shoes and an old flame

shopping today i see a pair of kinky
yves st. laurent
shoes and
think of you
now why do you
suppose my mind
not unlike bubble
gum pushed to its
very limits springs
back upon your image
sticking to the thought
of you wondering how
you'd feel about those
skinny call-girl heels cause
i'm still   coming on to you
you see   even though i
tell my-   self you're gone
now one   of those people we
speak   of with reverence or
a hint   of smile suggesting something
deeper   than we ever let on   your name
still   makes me smile and think of
high-   heel shoes-the higher, the better

1. Monte de las Piedras Rosas

There's a piñon tree outside
my window, full
of tiny silent verdins blending
into its sparse needles. I
wouldn't have noticed them
but one bird fluttered,
as if suddenly chilled,
its russet feathers like
an early sunset signaling
a change in season; then
the whole tree shuddered
and, a breath later, it is bare.

2. Los Alamos

Why the name? Not a poplar in sight.
Not a sapling, not a songbird. Not a soul.
In the circular distance
Las Truchas, implacable peaks (second
highest in New Mexico)
secure the sky to the land;
the pueblo bearing their name
reclining in the hollow of one slope—
waiting, watchful
of the encroaching barrenness below.

Crosses carved from the raw earth
lase lurid warnings across our path,
reminding us, *yes, this is the place*.

We drive past an old adobe hut. The face
of Christ, painted in a blaze
of reds and black across its whole facade,
looks back at us in pain and disbelief.

Los Alamos, Los Alamos,
sacred, secret origin of death—
the name explodes within my head,
dustblood settles on my eyelids, my tongue.

We slow down, as though searching for something,
something to still the shame.
A sign of hope, of purpose. Of forgiveness.

Silence. A dry silence. A dusty silence.

And in the shadow of the trading post,
half-hidden from the brutal sky,
sullen youngsters damn us with their eyes.

They do not wave as we drive by.

3. Promesas

To El Santuario de Chimayó,
as to the Ganges, they flock—
the needy, curious, doubting, and devout,
looking for a spiritual handout
from this "most holy national shrine"
(so named under the provisions,
of the Historic Sites Act of 1935).
They're coming "to witness, to commemorate
the history of the United States."
United States?—this here's MEXICO, hombre.

And I, the tourist, come too;
to pay homage, to honor—what?
A lost heritage? A dying legacy?
These strangers who speak my tongue
are not *my* people? I'm from Borinquen—
that tiny island drowning in a sea of Coca-Cola.
These people have their patria.

An old woman jesusiando follows
my pilgrimage into the dank, dark belly

of the sanctuary, her face parched
like the land she is condemned to till,
her fingers flitting from relic
to relic—touching, stroking,
needing to lay hands on her history, to feel
the pulse of her ancestral heart.
The walls are taut with hope and trust;
trinkets everywhere—charms, lockets,
wedding rings with tiny messages of love,
service medals, bracelets, dogtags—all
fabricating a haunting collage of life, death.
Of endurance. Ah yes, endurance.

A cabinet displays photographs of dear ones
with names like the sons in that old song:
Pedro, Pablo, Chucho, Jacinto y José; and
letters signed *tu hijo, tu hijita,*
tu marido que te quiere siempre.
Siempre—what a warped and wicked word!

In the center of the room
plastic icons adorned with rosary beads
remind me of deer heads
during the Zuni Shalako—
        turquoise and silver squash blossoms
        wrapped around their slender necks
        to ward off the evil eye of winter—
and in the corners, totemic,
canes and crutches and discarded casts.

And, finally, *promesas.* Tacked to the walls.
Hand written promises to God:

> *This cross is a symbol in thanking you*
> *for the safe return of my son Juan*
> *from combat duty in Vietnam.*
> *I made a promise to walk 150 miles*
> *from Grants, New Mexico, to Chimayó.*

But what if Juan had not come back—what then?
Would his father have dissolved the covenant,

his rage propelling him to curse his God?
Or would he have submitted—
walking farther, seeking deliverance?

It's what my grandfather would have done.
I remember now, I am six, sickly.
My grandfather on his knees beside my bed.
I remember the promised curls
cascading down his chest
and over his vest like a tabard.   Once
in a dream, I felt them soft against my cheek
and woke up weeping.

"Kitsch!" quips a man behind me.

The light outside is blinding.

4. Chimayó

A dog ambles across the empty dusty road
lifting his hind leg to pee on the garbage cans
of El Chimayó Café where

BURRITOS * TACOS
HAMBURGERS
Y
GAS

are sold. Round brown faces framed by crudely
lettered signs—a pink OPEN above,
COCA COLA in chartreuse below—peer out at us
from the concession stand as we drive up.
On the adobe a painted hotdog trickles
crusty catsup and relish. We stop. Wait for gas.
Suddenly a car pulls up behind
imprisoning us in the past. A woman cautions
¡Mira—tengan cuidado!
Pointing to our captor, she motions
little circles around her temples and mouths

loco, loco,
esperen hasta que se vaya.

Dogs in slow motion—salivating, panting
like weary wolves—stop traffic as they sprawl
themselves across the road and lick their genitals.

Down here,
a brilliant heat subdues the evening,
while in the mountains, always the rain
falling in smudged streaks
like mammoth shades to earth

and always God hiding
behind every dwarfed juniper bush, chamiza,
ready to spring on smug Anglo skepticism
with some special sleight of hand—now
a simple dandelion, now a raspberry finch, all
ingeniously framed by a motionless sky
the blue of my youngest child's eyes.

And far in the background a Rothko mural
of muted mountains surrounds us
with peaks of brooding greens, grays, lavenders
lapping and overlapping. And always *there*
the hills, and always *here* the center, my center,
extending outward past the past,
far beyond the future—
for I was here before, even before
I drank the magic Chimayó potion
that obliterates time and space and boundaries,
restoring peace, oneness.

I am the bear that comes at nightfall
to greet the new moon
soy india, soy mexicana
soy mujer
soy

5. Return to the City of Holy Faith

Signs back to Santa Fe are incongruous,
out of sync with this timeless world

Shirley's Pizza Parlor
Nambé Bronze Works
ICE
What do I know of bronze and ice?
I'm of another age.

I want to tuck myself into a fold
of a withered speckled mossgreen mountain
and write my Latino soul's secrets
for my children
who may otherwise never know *me.*

Lightning like an arrow to an enemy heart
points the way home.
¡Mierda! It's raining in Santa Fe.
(My holy faith is being tested again.)
I still have to pack and catch the 7:15 flight home.
Home? I *am* home.

A final look.

The natives of Santa Fe know their place—
low earth homes blending with the clay ground.
They know the servants of the Lord
do not compete. They support the heavens
as do my hands when into evening
I reach up and cup the trembling stars.

We drive by a graveyard of unknown
New Mexican soldiers, their bravery
squeezed parenthetically between two insults—
BONANZA CITY on the left, USED CARS
on the right. Where in hell am I?
St. Francis Drive, the answer. *To the hills!*

Away! Away! A las montañas,
like Carlos, my fugitive uncle,
the Puerto Rican banner
tucked resolutely beneath his arm—
defying windmills, imperialism, death. *Away!*

COLLECTING LAST LOOKS

I'm returning, cramped with curiosity
to images of family

and distant friends—deviled
from years of years of homework and tests

cajoling to have catch up conversations
over stiff umbrella drinks and Tito's

congas and timbales or Celia's "Azúcar"
creating warm and pulsating Miami laughter.

I'm sprinkling goodbyes by the thimblefuls
to new acquaintances—etching

etching their faces into my memory.
A Picasso carving

—priceless; pillaged
after graduation.

MIS MIL Y UNA NOCHES

I release you on American Lit
and College Algebra days
when my thoughts are consumed
with linear equations, chapters,

lists of characters and essays.
And the brush of your pomegranate lips
denied lengthens the hours
and lessens my fashion sense.

I release you on sultry sangria nights:
congas and timbales, guiras and
accordions providing reasons for
me to whisper my desires and dedicate

mimosa kisses to your neckline—
to paso doble or rumba
with the semblance of your embrace,
the trace of your rosewater fragrance.

I release you with a 1001 good-byes
for these 1001 nights, with a vow to return
in your dreams or mine or
when you learn to love me.

I release you like a soldier going off
to war, with an indefinite timeframe
for a promise which may go un-
kept.

I release you wearing the Ohio State
University t-shirt you gave me
on your last visit.
Calling you less,yet speaking to you more.

Seeing you less & less, yet more & more
you accompany me on my morning
walks, breathing life's blessings in
—you lay with me on unfurnished

living room or bedroom floors listening
to Ray Charles, Lionel Richie
or enjoying the night's stillness
with quiet reflection.

I release you on dirty laundry days:
$1.50 per load, 25c every eight minutes
to dry—yet the t-shirt I wash by hand—
on the rocks of the Missouri which learned

our names, with the sensual breezes
which witnessed our ardent glances, blushed
at our succulent words & drifted
them like dandelions towards one another.

I release you memorizing every string
of fabric onto my person, absorbing
every vestige of you which remains;
one beguiling wear, one agonizing wash

one barbaric sunrise at a time.

TÍA LICHA'S HOUSE

What I remember? I remember at four years of age
Tía Licha told me to stop—
white sheets, yellow stains.

At twelve, opening iron gates, hand in hand,
tía rubbing index finger on my palm
saying, "This is how you get a girl to sleep with you."

Tía's house invokes memories of cherry scents,
of extreme heat, mosquito nets, outdoor latrines,
night time bed pans, and of waste cans filled
with cutting water.

Who says that something dirty can't be beautiful?
Who says dirty thoughts can't be innocent?

The pipes run water. Electricity lasts
twenty hours or more. She has a kitten now,
and most days there's food enough for two.

I bought you more passion fruit juice. I'm leaving
the bathroom with the Cosmo's,
and that towel stained with hyacinth untouched; it always drowned
the squalor. Everything is a dusted smile.

What happened to our Pledge?

I'll check under the sink; something about the lemon
scent and its twilight setting that makes gathering shadows
less of a chore. This reminds me, I'm leaving the laundry dirty
since you believe I ruined your sweetest taboo. Down
the hall past pictures of family and of our first
trip to Graceland for Sadina's wedding—Bon Jovi plays.

It's a quarter to 5, and wanting to be gone before you get home, I abandon
all hopes for hospital corners and extra fluffy pillows. Closing
the door behind me, singing,

"Shot through the heart and you're to blame,
you give love a bad name."

WE STARTED A CONVERSATION

During a time when heartbroken & lost
—hope
was pondering in my soul

when with sunlight & rain
seeds I've sown
were coming into fruition
&

untamed ambition
coupled w/a broken bond
found me timid
w/love

yet she
nectarine smile, violet voice,
timely sent—
conspiring to fulfill God's design
permitted the alignment
so that our planets
may collide.

Her Earth me my Jupiter
amidst a desert of stars
and I understood the physics
of things
—though she retained
her mystery.

And I though lacking
endeavored to keep her
w/in my reach,
to decipher
every syllable her nature speaks
& fall asleep to the rustling
of her leaves—

Hoping nothing concerning her

gets lost in translation

we started a conversation
during which I've experienced
a metamorphosis of sorts.

What once a caterpillar heart
has revealed itself a butterfly
in her eyes

and though
wings outstretched
gaze piercing her horizon,
an indigo haze thwarts
my ascension

making me wary
of her tempest touch.

Unable to adjust
to feelings of wanting to fall
& in her wind take flight
to follow the call
and manifest to life

the image she sees of me
which is merely
a reflection
of the splendor I behold

& though often times her waning moods
I can't control

We started a conversation
During a time when heartbroken & lost.
Now—hope
is pondering in my
soul.

A-7

I saw page 7
Of the Daily Paper

29 graves
Home to the bodies of 29

Daughters
Mothers
Sisters
Lovers

Workers

The walk home from the maquiladora
was long

Is long

Her death
Buried beneath the weather
News From Washington
News from anywhere

But the news from right over the fence

A-7

Close enough to notice
Buried deep enough to forget

FANTASMA

Los colores flash fantastic
Azul sky
Amarillo sun
washed down with horchata

Irish Whiskey bleeds
All over my American Dream
but nightmares prevail
on my neighbor's family tree

Pendejos post up on my block
¿Que onda güey?
Mother Fucker, I've been here
for an eternity,
go be a stereotype in the suburbs,
I've got Chavez on my mind.

THE WHEELS ON THE BUS

Buried in stacked shadows of apartment complexes
We played in the desert that was once a cemetery
Jumping off gravestones—
        Remember when we found that bone?

Riding make shift bikes, down make shift trails
I remember doing anything
                    to stretch daylight   escape home

Too young to be left alone   we rode
 the metro from sun up   until mom came home
Singing with drunks, an old woman who gave us candy
We secretly called her bruja   you
                secretly wanted her to take you home

This was summer for us   El Paso
days wandering our hometown
pressed firmly   between   hot sun and pavement
We came home with big enough dreams
                                        to last the school year

LA PRIMERA MAÑANA

Tangas in the morning sounds like roosters
Unceasingly calling us to a new day
They wake up before the songbirds begin
A carcacha races by en la calle
The smell of smoke from the mountains
Floats in
Like incense at Mass
A mist veils the mountains
Soon to be revealed as the day takes form
Brushed in the canvas of the morning sky
A splash of pink where the sun will soon appear

Now I know my directions
Forget about east, west, north and south
Forget what time it is
The sight, sound and smell of this pueblito
Will lead me

PRAYER BEFORE MEALS

I'm stepping out of the kitchen
and into my career

Mom has pushed me
Grandma has prayed for me

Grandma made tortillas every day
Mom taught her father English

I'm going to eat the world

SECRET ANTI-AGING FORMULA

Her skin never wrinkled
And I used to wonder why

Her skin never wrinkled
As every year passed by

Look at Grandma's hands my mom would say
I bet you'd never think of how they stay that way

As she grew older
Her skin remained smooth and tan

Even when she passed
She had the most youthful hands

I wish I could bottle
And sell this answer to smooth skin

I'd sell it at Nordstrom's
And call it "Hands of a Mexican"

Her skin never wrinkled
And now I know the secret

It was her tortilla recipe
And the manteca she used in it

Corridos, baladas y cumbias blaring from passing cars accent the air

See the way of life. Compadres y comadres gathered in front of the other's homes. Chicos on motor scooters. Mothers with babies, headed to La Plaza. There's the "Buenos días," "buenas tardes" and "buenas noches" as you pass one another.

See the milagros encased at the foot of each statue in the church. A cured leg, arm and spirit show you how faith heals. The Virgen gazes toward the heavens as she crushes the head of the serpent.

Smell the fresh jugo de mango, manzana y naranja. Mixed together or by itself. Chile, sal y limón make pepinos y cocos taste like more than cucumbers and coconuts.

Mountains surround you in the pueblito, weave you into the pace of solace and pepper your English with words and phrases.

When a voice is muted, the senses take over. Ándale pues. . .

DEATH THEMES

There were walls, and flowers,
stone and broken glass. I
swept the dust and the litter
left behind, and sat to bring her
the week's news. She, like always,
listened in silence, and I could feel
her head nod or shake
when the buses drove by.
My mother, even in life, carried
a tombstone around her neck:
　　　　Let my arms reach out like tree limbs
　　　　and my feet dig deep like roots,
　　　　so that my children may climb them
　　　　and speak with God at the top.

TREMBLING

if allowed,
 i would drink from the cup of your chest
 until i lost my balance and my eyesight.

if prompted,
 i would become the pouncing feline, the steady pendulum,
 the morning elixir, the remaining mist after dawn.

if i could run,
 i would chase you down
 the streets of this broken kingdom until your
knees gave out and you were forced to ask:
fix them.

there is a thin line between tragedy
 and ecstasy.
 one can, with care, walk it.

if i could choose,
 i would scribble you down on the margins of my lips
 and whistle out my bedroom windows
 until ink whirlwinds scattered you all over the lawn.

AT THE WATER'S EDGE

You wonder why they come
from so far away
to walk along the edge
I have wondered too
my back to the ground
my feet sinking in the sand
the water inching to my toes

And it comes to me
how young I was
before I saw the sea

I remember sun and wind
and her screams above the foam
I see the roll wrap itself
along the wide reach of my eyes
I see the glint just at my feet
after the water's rinse

I chase it
as it rolls and tumbles
on the tossed floor
I reach it
as her screams and waves embrace
somewhere above my head

I hold it just before
tumbled broken rinsed and spewed
twirling across the sand
and my empty outstretched hand

For years I tell her
I held a piece of gold tight
For years she tells me
we are never so blessed
as to lose the things
we have left behind
or to survive clean
the water's determined rinse

BITTER SUITE

Prologue

Fall is a hunger
that lingers
long past winter
The canopies are strewn about
The squirrels in a mad dash
gather and hide
what in a few days
they will have forgotten
Then they will sit and wait
for the seed that fills the feeders

I.

The winds have changed
In the morning
the briskness cuts
easy through the fabric
and with its fingers
trails across my back
I see the wind play its games
I see it run squirrel
and shake the leaves and dry branches
to the ground
It soars up the naked trunks
and slaps the tops
It sends sparrows and ravens
down into the shelter of the creaking barn
In the swaying afternoon
the grayness of night approaching
it drops a shower of rotting leaves
to cascade about my feet
It gathers itself and lurks
at the edges of the woods
and in a sudden rush
embraces me

Take me

It only snaps its tail
across my face and leaves
laughing as it winds up the trunks
and tickles the remaining leaves
on the balding crowns
It jumps down to the lower branches
hugging from lesser trunk
to lesser trunk
It is a smile on the naked redbuds
as it tweaks the tips
Then it is gone
a tumble of leaves
spiraling along the ground

In the stillness
the sun fades in lazy fits
and lights the droplets
falling random upon my cheeks

II.

Out of the garden
the patch and the orchard
Past the gate
firmly set in the brick
cold wind and rain
take me step and step
Another gate another space
And a path that wends
back upon itself

See the stone on the ground
The stone lies heavy on the plot
Lift up the stone
Call it here
Bring it easy
Find the notes
Something that will move it
I will sing and it will fly

Graceful is the flight of the stone
Singing lift all the other stones
Stack them one on top of the other
Watch the notes bend and resonate
Stones like figure eights
bouncing along the taut lines.

The air is still
Still
the air is still

III.

Think to the middle
of a cool breeze blowing
gentle across the face
of a girl with flowers in her hair
She dreams of temples in the air
She turns to me
Who are you
I am a builder of temples in the air
in the still air

Girl turn to me
Girl turn to the me that sings
See
An edge forms here
Nothing tumbles here
The stones that form the edge
have made our bed
Come lie with me
Wait nothing
think nothing
but the grace of a song
on a wave of air stirring
the building of an altar
a temple in the air

Come here girl let us dance
You on that corner and me here

Twirl twirl and twirl
turn to me your eyes
and your darkening hair
Open your arms
I will come to you
You make the first move
I will make the last

Open up
The air is moving
stones are flying
The sweat that forms about my brow
drips drips slow
rivulets upon the ground

You turn and catch my eye
                    Give it back
Turn and catch my breath
                    Give it back
My heart tumbles to your feet
                    Give it back
At the corner
the movement of your skirt
the turn of your heels
high in the air
                    Give it back
The brush of your lashes
across my cheeks
The taste of your berry tongue
upon my lips
                    Give it back
                    Give it back

IV.

Falling into your eyes
I kiss your berry lips
and out into the silent streets
my sonorous voice
joyous and loud above the multitudes
gathered in church pews

I sing to the rafters
Stones fly with me
Sparrows sing canary

I am scale melody and counterpoint
joy in the upper and lower registers
a bridge affirming
a coda
I am dissonance and consonance
in a communal choir
I am chaos harmonious

The period to a raging storm
I am tamer of winds and wills
of days nights and dreams
As I am so is the world

I am the gift given
the gift accepted

V.

Fall is a hunger that lingers long past winter

I walk slow to the sound ahead of us
Are you there
so light in the back
Do I hear you in the path
Don't look back
The losing is in the looking
I am afraid of nonexistent
steps behind my shadow
Up ahead the light that is swelling
Behind
barely a whisper
Are you there
Do you see me

I am a beard
grown gray on a sad face

in a tight room with drawn shades
lit by a candle that flickers seconds away
above a Greek diner that opens all night

And you so timid to others
a raging storm in my center
Strain for the light
I promise a world
The opening is here
the entrance waits

Are you there

VI.

The end of the day comes in the beginning
In the tick tick tick
of a counter reset and reset and reset
until a cognizant smile breaks
on the corners of a drawn face
a face that knows me but turns
afraid to take a chance
And the day ends in the sun
on a park bench at noon
with pigeons huddled on bread crumbs
with the north wind spitting gusts in the fall
as the leaves brown
Tick Tick Tick Talk
And the day ends in the shadows
of a face dissolving
with my arm about an aura
whose substance fades
to a capricious whim

I turn turn turn
slow to the anger that swells
Don't resign
I am not others
I am I
Take a chance girl

take a chance
Don't
turn turn turn away

VII.

Out of the garden
past the gate
firmly set in the brick
another space and other steps
steps that turn to themselves
and return to the start
that ends at the door
of a window that closes

Hear a laugh receding
like a love dreamt
See a woman alone
in the stillness passing
from today to tomorrow
inexorable
unattended

In the still air the stones
fall flat around the plot
and your name heavy and straight
is etched on the graying rock

VIII.

Tomorrow comes tonight
timid to the touch

There is nothing to be found
A corpse
a shoe
the hem of a skirt
the trace of a smile
the squeeze of a hand

One breath and the closing of a door

A photograph
Too many and not one
A soul
a purple aster
withered in a smoked glass vase

Your hand scratching
slowly down my back
No back
No rolling onto you
No falling on the floor
Or the cascade of pillows
beneath the fan
Or the rustle of the sheets

A gust of heather
and the clacking of a shoe
Once only
The rustle of the bags
Too many and not one
Or the half skips and
clucks across the floor
The plié and pirouette to a stop
with the hands thrust to the side

There is nothing to be found

No pirouettes across the floor
No pirouettes across
No pirouettes at all

IX.

Think of a memory
easily forgotten
Think of a tryst in a cold room
and the words not spoken
The long sleep furtively taken
The nights of hiding

and the passion of time
Backwards
Back to the beginning
of a dull sensation in the groin
an ember that strains for the wind
that whistles above a scream in a closet
of walls caving and the urine
that hangs in the air
the legs bent and wound
tight to the stomach

Think of a hunger that lingers
A malignant embrace that festers
and attaches carrion on a life long passage
A cure that kills and a redemption that curses

Come boys
melodies for the taking
Pick a name and I will extend it to night
and in your lover's arms you will awaken
Silly girls
all of a piece and for making
Don't promise what morning will change
You leave off better the one
that will embrace you tonight
than the one that in the morning awaits you
better in the arms
that barely embrace you
than the mood turned reverential
and the familial that kills you

I am craftsman and nothing defines me divine
I am a gift given a gift wasted
with no purpose no direction
set in the street with a power that blinds me

X.

In the measure of a life
a string wends through the center

A careening nothing
pulling pushing
tying things into a knot
The night takes drink
from the parched ground
dribbles drops past blistered lips
I am thirsty
This is not a comfortable bed
It should face the courtyard
where the sun breaks
and in the dawn
frames the open window
In a moment there will be
pictures on the wall
music in the air
laughter on the floor
In a moment
there will be someone
out of the darkness
with their eyes wide shut
and he will say
Come follow me again and again
In that moment
I will know you
know me.

XI.

The red sun catches the spigot
as it dribbles a constant flow
that pools onto the muddy floor
The ravens flutter to the edge
and shake the drizzle
a raucous splash
in the waning afternoon

I step to the water's edge
and sink into the cool mud
See the water that overflows the pool
See it trickle along the path

I step light
step by step
And as I walk along the path
that brings me from the bath
with my eyes cast on the rotting mulch
that fills the space between the logs
I find the berry with its red coat
buried in the folds of the ivy
I reach and gently pull
to where it comes into my hand
I draw it to my mouth
I am struck by the bitter sweetness
Here in late fall a strawberry fruits
and dissolves behind my eager lips

Once
They called me the strawberry boy
and with my basket full
in the high measure
of a melodious spring
found me
wild
as the west wind on the skin
certain
as the morning dew on the lilac sprig
come to feed you strawberries
one by one
Sweet
as an expectant kiss

Do you hear them calling
Bring on the baskets boys
Here in this patch there is fruit aplenty
Come boys take them to your sweethearts
Put a strawberry to her mouth
Watch the fruit as it disappears behind her lips
See the smile and the turn of the eyes
as they come to rest on you
Hear the lips that caress your name
Take another love

Take another love
Take another love
I bring a full basket

XII.

The wind at the edges lurks and frets
and whips itself into a rage
It darts across the checkered cover
of the oaks and sycamores
and swirls into a tempest
on the flooding floor

The spigot strains and breaks
The water cascades in falls across the path
and the ground bleeds berries
as far as the earth can see

And I am a picker of berries
Another hand
and another handful
And the bosom of my shirt swells red
Wait love
Wait
I gather the first of this year's crop

XIII.

Age time and wind wither their histories
on the stones that litter the silent plots

In the shade of a day grown long
a youth grown old
a time grown weary
a flickering light disappearing
By the graying stones
akimbo on the fresh dead lawn
engulfed by the raging winds
that claw the swaying trunks

On a mound just off the path
that wends about
I sit and wait
with a full basket in my arms
And if darkness
gives one more chance
find me here love
again and again
come back for you
until I get it right

THE LADIES OF THE RAPHAEL

Good night ladies
Good night
Solid in your distance
opposite the winding drive
balanced against the banisters
The doorman in his burgundies
bores the hip night
The distant laughter
spry legs on the crosswalks
Smiles with destinations
and discoveries
The light of the cars
Forward
No turn
Not stop
No memory
Headlong to a swinging night
while a harsh light ripples
over the silent shouts of women
long accustomed to smiles
Lulla lulla lullaby
Goodnight ladies
Good night

MALVERN HILL

The branches have dropped to the ground
heavy with the cold rain's bracelets

The stalls are closed
The wind whistles through the trestles
still in need of a fresh coat of paint
The hands that fumbled at the table
with the bread crumbs in her fingers
have disappeared

When I last saw her
she was riding a horse bareback
hard into the wind and the night
There goes a girl
with a particular affliction
She sleeps hard upon the pillows

I slough off to the only bed I know
the only familiar that wakens me

I am not the I
not the I that you would think.

I
gather up the straw
that falls about
and make whole a man
with no reflection

I
set out to see the yesterdays
that passed me by
through the smoke
burning in the eyes
through the pages
littered on the floor
and the messages not read
the calls not returned

the letters not sent
or written
or thought upon
or the ashtrays
overflowing on the dusty sill

And the door
that constant creak that sounds
only when I leave and enter
and the rug worn and bare
to the splintered floor
and the many layers of paint
fallen to the ground
among the papers that pile up
with the sameness of the toss
and the sameness
of the letters and the words

I am I
at the border
I
at the sides
I
at the rail
like a guilty witness
to a murder

My death
a silent falling down
down to the crushing
bending of the legs
and the stiffness of the joints
cramped and crimped
till useless to the neighbors

I carry myself like a gentle man
with my white flowing hair
my face hard into the wind
disdainful of a cane
not a crutch to anyone
no help to anyone

No one waits for me
and I wait for no one

Except for her

That girl that fell
down the dried river bed
as she careened past the summer stalls
and gathered all the color
swept it into the folds of her apron
and tucked the rest neatly in her bonnet

She fell down into a hole
Her rose drawn cheeks
fixed their eyes on me
She yelled help me please
You there a crutch to no one
No help to anyone

I saw her fall
and no one came for her

I went no further
then the startled rush
of feathers in a swamp
at the falling of a pebble
into a shallow cove

I saw the crime
and did not report it
Who would listen
and to what would I relate
a girl tumbling rolling
with summer stuffed into a picnic basket
and a pomegranate in her hand

I know where she rests
but I will not go there
I am not a master of the arts
I am a blessed observer
and a quiet one at that

IN THE SIMPLEST OF WAYS

At Saqharra you crossed my path
walking along the causeway
out of the columned halls
the black veil across your mouth
the length of your shadow
as it brushed against my knee

You walked onto the portico
outside Olympic House
You came on a breeze
The dates lost some of their leaves
You picked the bougainvillea
and tucked it to your hair

On the boat from Piraeus to Siros
with the setting sun
on the temple of Poseidon
you stood at the rail
with the sun cast halos
and the wind's smooth caress

It was you on a white horse
crossed the Ponte Vecchio
with the half turned smile
of a girl retreating to a dream
While lovers stole their kisses
I held the reins for the king

Off the Place de la Concorde
on the darkened street
with speeding cars between
you stood and looked at me
then twirled and twirled and
dissolved into the rushing lights

It was in your hand
the curl of your fingers
the smile that drew me to the bench

Sitting beneath O'Higgins' statue
my eyes to the pockmarked stones
while mimes told the news

It was you at La Recolletta
darting out of the mausoleums
a cat in your hands
Evita's flowers in your teeth
You danced the tango
while I sat quiet in my seat

In the vaulted cathedral
your brown smile is wide
in the flicker of the candles
as I
lazy in a hammock by the bay
by the cliffs falling to the sea
hope to meet you again
in the simplest of ways

THE WATER MOVES IN CIRCLES ABOUT MY SPEECH

We launch canoes of birch
and willow seats and oak paddles
with ochres and reds painted on the sides
A measured humming into the water

The flowing ribbon of the stream
gray and silver
slow and winding

The wind sifts through the trees
a plaintive whistle out into the cold
Far above other winds move
thermals rising from the springs

Hawks and eagles soar
in escalator moments
high and easy to the sky

The buzzards hover
float to the branches
and quietly note the passing

A hawk moves along the water's edge
from Washington to Hermann
past New Haven

We edge the prow closer to the bank
In the hollow of a sandbar
build a fire dim against the stars
We ease catfish
and cornbread crumble
gentle into the grease

The darkening wraps about my dreams
I respond by drawing the blanket tighter
And curling the body deep into the folds

The valleys rills and springs
and the folding of the hills
into a crumpled comforter
bunched on a stiff mattress

The flowing ribbon of the stream
gray and silver
slow and winding

Through the night
the drops hit hard and steady
against matted ground
Soon puddles breach the mounds
sandbars shift
till constant in their inconstancy

We curse the mud make our way to shore
On the banks with the houses high on stilts
we sit with the dogs barking
We watch the water wrap about the land
and separate banks into islands
and fields gray to the edge
The logs that raged through the night
on the bank crash and whittle

See the boats labor in the eddies
fret into the currents
barges cut and strewn across lawns
docks floating just above the rippled edges
The piles that gouge
pout into the river
And the hills above roots
that dig deep into the dirt
release the red earth into the rushing water

See trunks tossed like bridges
across widening banks
And the water laces
above and beneath
wraps memory in haze

The flowing ribbon of the stream
gray and silver
slow and winding

Rotting hulks of houses
cars leaching poison to the ground
Hands rush to the water's edge
once more for cleansing

See the flocks of geese migrate
slow down the careening edge
They will be a long time arriving
Somewhere horses thunder
distant on the hills

Rabbits and squirrels stop
see the naked season
surrender quickly
burrow deeper
into cellars and basements

There is nothing in the passing
that has not passed in the measuring
And leaving is just that
the movement from one moment to another
with no trace of embarrassment

The sun rises in blinks into the sky
Water pools become
drizzles in the afternoons
With the first nights come
redbirds and flags waving in the air

The whistle of the train
marks the distance
from the small bedrooms
side by side along the track
to the glow of the bodies
warm and safe
The evening's new arrivals

huddle inside the fires
raging in a square

Around a leafless standing oak
pictures and letters
and curios on a shelf
form floes and oxbows
break the shelter
shunt the storm
And everywhere
the land's acceptance
and the rolling over

New rivers and streams will flow
and when time has reclaimed us
some will not see the stitching
and the rocks witnessing
and the defiles into the earth

Some will not walk across the wideness
that stretches into miles
Some will not watch the flocks
that fly and tire
when they reach the other side

The train whistles us away
The whining at the curbs
becomes moments fast in passing
things left so far behind
in a diary burning in the light
Past and above the flattened homes
that shape the air and slam the winds
Past stones that frame the bulging hillocks
and the cut wild grasses tamed to a height
that barely touches the playful breezes

Follow the bent signposts
hidden meanings and designs
Ride along the byways
the destination all planned out

Let trains climb high into the plains
and away from the cliffs and water
Let us go to where the rhythms
long since gave way
to beats bangs regrets

The flowing ribbon of the stream
gray and silver
slow and winding

From on high
the wind sun and folded horizons
tumbled rolled and wrinkled
like discarded towels
weave a gypsy symmetry
and we are vagabonds
once removed from the bank

We will take the measure of the movement
to make the incomplete sentences
like faded orange balls
strung across power lines
where a bridge once spanned
from one shore to another

What will I do
in a blood red moon
in a high season
with the waters
coursing over the dikes
and the train stations full
the whistle of the train
silent across the flooded fields

And the waters that move
in circles about my speech

WHAT DO YOU LOOK FOR LOVE

What do you look for love
in the mornings when you wake
or the nights when you dream
The signs that will come
and knock you to the ground
to be smitten
when all desires to give in
are foreign to your nature
How will the rocking come
when your hands and feet
are so steady to the floor

You ask more of the world
than it can give
All the planets must align
following the arc of a full eclipse
hawks and eagles in unison soar
and ladybugs and butterflies
fly and crawl in pilgrimage
to your door
Five stars must end every horoscope
and the lines of the I-Ching
and the tarot cards
blind prophets in the street
and psychics on the screen
must all agree
The gray clouds that hover
must part
and the sun's light
shine the name of the one
written clearly at your feet

Then celestial choirs
of hosannas and hallelujahs
will fill the air
and cherubim and seraphim
will blow the trumpets high

and everywhere
goodwill will fill the void
and nations for a second will stop
hold their breath and weep
that the cosmos has found
the one you seek
Oh that the world were so
and if it were
that I would be the one
so clearly writ

But if not me
and all this should come to pass
what marvel it would be
to see the universe
in such conspiracy

WHEN THE WIND IS SLIGHT

When the wind is slight and cool
the birds full about the feeders
and the seed plentiful
that it overflows to the ground
and the squirrels gathered
with plenty at their feet
to grouse about

And the buds just formed
begin to leaf into the fullness
that obscures the branches
the grass high enough
to catch the early morning breeze
and the silence
that comes over the hills
settling over the houses of the city

She will sit quietly at my side
sipping her coffee
with the morning paper on her lap
and it will feel
like everything fits
the light sweater
the spring morning air
the trace of the sun
that lazy burns away the fog

Yet it will come
crawling beneath the grass
burrowing close to my feet
a thin finger scratching
at the tips of my toes
a coldness creeping
up the tightening calves
slipping into the bones
coursing up my crooked back
reaching to the nape

beginning a massage
that steals my breath

And in the garden
in the breeze that flips
the pages easy on my lover's knees
I will become bones in a chair
with the worms
blithely twirling at my feet

What is the matter she will ask
Nothing I will tell her
There must have been a hint of winter
in this early spring air
And I will close my eyes and wait
the nothing
I know is always there

ONE MORE SUMMER

Amá, I can go one more summer.
One more summer me voy a las piscas. ¡No más!
Y luego I go to college. A Yale.
Not jail, Amá. YALE ... al Norte.
Me dieron un scholarship. They'll pay my way to college.
Then I'll never have to go las piscas again.
Ni tu tampoco, Amá. I'll take care of you.
Just one more summer, Amá.
Just one more summer to earn money for clothes.
And money to come back and see you en Krismas.
No, I'll never forget you, Amá, or your tamales de Krismas
ni tus buñuelos de año nuevo.
Just one more summer, Amá.
One more summer.

Mi hijo, como te extraño.
Tu carita, tus ojos negros brillantes. Tu risa y tus travesuras.
Y tu en el Norte. Estás en el Norte.
Y en el Valle la vida sigue:
La que era tu novia se casó.
Y tu mejor amigo ahora es manager del H.E.B..
Y yo, aquí. Mirando hacia el norte .¿Como me decías?
Just one more summer, Amá. Just one more summer.
Y así le digo a Dios, que quiero
just one more summer con mi hijo.
One more summer.

SEPTEMBER 1957

I grasp her hand with my small brown one
My lifeline to all I know
She releases my hand and gives me a gentle nudge
Away from her toward all things I do not know
She waves goodbye as the gaping door
Swallows me...

First day of school

CONSIDERING OCEANS

I

Inside the museum this sultry afternoon,
the air-conditioned hum offers an imitation
peace like that of libraries and empty churches.
I wait for you, as I have promised,
promising myself this afternoon will do no damage
to an earlier oath, watching out the window
where the sun shatters
against the fountain's water and water
transmutes to something other than air or water.
Though I sit at the point of betrayal,
my face feels smooth and unyielding
as the face of Saint Teresa
gilded on peeling wood or the sea
on the wall before me, becalmed yet broken
by the ship's hull and dorsal fins.
The ocean next to that one is all drowning
storm and cloud, as if the two paintings were
before and after, the seeds of one
hidden in the other.

II

Must it always be one or the other?
My husband's love laps at my closed shore,
then slides back into turquoise depths, a lake
his love, no sea like yours,
gray ocean breakers rolling over
galleons and frigates and the backs of whales
and sharks and squid and dolphins who
leap and squeal as they follow the sails
of men (and now their motors), catching rides
on the wakes of ships. He has no dolphins
in him, only freshwater fish, frogs and trees
under the water, a sunken forest
drowned with its squirrels, snakes, ants and bees
that once made a world, reduced
to a floating green crest.

III
We whisper in deep-carved shadows
of the recreated medieval chapel.
They built to keep the heat and sun out.
The dark ages knew
summer draws insanity and sin,
a poultice pulling infection from the soul
to burst in the sun.
It was always summer in Eden.

IV
Mother of Perpetual Help,
with your slanted eyes hurt
by visions of your later Son
who sits now, infant, in your hand, a perfect
fit, and takes your thumb
between his palms, as if to suck,
pray for us.

Mother of the Word Incarnate,
though attended by angels
floating near your narrow ears,
though surrounded by hieroglyphics
and striped everywhere,
your Son as well, with gold,
though you wear a halo crown,
despise not our petitions.

Virgin of Virgins,
in paint, wood, song, stone, clay,
I stand before this incarnation
with its blue porcelain necklace
and long hands that cup your Infant
as if you would never let go.
Help us, we pray.

V
We enter the twentieth century
on the floor above. Neon tubes,

gears and ratchets, kinetic
sculptures flashing dissonance,
disjointed collage, counterfeit
museum guard so real
you ask for directions to the men's room,
have to get them from the small black
woman in uniform in the corner.
I turn back,
down the marble stairs,
run through the Egyptians
all the way to the Coptics, hide
among flat-faced icons, holding my breath
from fear of your finding me,
of what I will want to do
if you do. I watch you pass the massive stone
lion-casket on your way out.
I breathe again
in pain.

VI
In these halls of art, Mother,
I call on you with your human face
and divine Lover who came
only once, leaving you to someone else's
kindness. I can see how hard
your life must have been with him
always forgiving.
Yet he loved the boy.
Of course, you were innocent,
they say, and angels smoothed
your way with Joseph afterward. None of them
will come to my husband, asleep,
to tell him I've escaped burning
but not the ocean.

VII
Am I any less lost in the storm
because it has a frame?
The Englishman who laid down
the paint so long ago felt
the lash of rain, shivered to thunder's
blast, saw lightning burn
its way across the clouds to the sea,
even if he stood before a tea table
on floral carpet as he splashed ocean
across canvas. His tempest rages before me
six generations later. Drenched,
I wander home.

BLAME IT ON SUMMER

that I smile too widely,
grinning really, and laugh
too loud and often; that I walk
with spring and sensual sway;
that I stretch myself and twist
like a cat
baking in the backyard
brightness; that my brain is sun-bleached,
all rule and thought boiled away, leaving
only sensory steam;
that my feverish eyes see strange dancing
flames in afternoon shadows
along the sides of streets and Bedouin oases, fragrant
with dates and goats and acrid desert waters,
in every suburban garden we pass
while you argue and drive
and I stare, heavy-brained with heat
and too aware of my own body
and every other;
that I take a lover,
brazenly, crazily,
too sun-stupid to be careful,
in my dreams.

CALACA COMEDY CENTRAL

In this time of marigolds and mariposas,
calacas, calaveras, and candles everywhere,
in this time when the veil between the worlds,
living and dead, is stretched thinnest,
watch the souls streaming through the tears,
trailing that unnatural chill of Lord Death's land.

Here he comes himself, skeleton jester,
with crown and scepter to beg
for the taste of mezcal y pan de muerto.
Dress him up for photos,
Lord Death just bares his teeth
in an everlasting grin and dances,
loose-limbed and clacking, bone on bone,
holding out his sombrero at the end
as he mimics a hacendado's formal bow.

Who knew he was such a comedian?
All our legends tell a different story,
scary and grim, not this grinning,
fingerbone-snapping prankster.
Who knew he could be so funny,
prancing around in silly costumes,
telling knock, knock jokes,
juggling sugar skulls,
striking ridiculous poses?

Be generous to that hat he passes
when his performance is finished.
No small change or paper bills.
This bony clown performs for one pay only,
a taste of what we take for granted
every day, a mouthful of mole,
a kiss, a look at the sunlight,
a breath of air like sweet wine,
one heartbeat rubbing up against another.

Once a year,
he comes to remind us
that life is a slapstick farce,
and his skeletal leer
is the ultimate punchline.

DREAMING OF MY LATE MOTHER-IN-LAW'S HOUSE

Smelling the sharp incense,
cumin and jalapeños,
I cross her floors
again, gold and white shag leading
past couch-flowers.
The television, an altar, always holds
fourteen family faces,
purple candles and Our Lady
of Guadalupe.

In the dining room,
Christ, crucified,
oversees holiday feasts,
and the corner between two doorways
holds the celebrant's chair
with gilded legs. Her sight
stolen by diabetes, Jennie
swivels—never rocks—from voice to voice,
answering with a high laugh like a child's
in an empty choirloft,
offering counsel and comfort
with a flutter of dove-plump hands.

Thermostats set at eighty
make sleep slow to come
in her high beds
while dried palm fronds, blessed
on Passion Sunday,
rattle against the lintels
and hold our city souls
inviolate
in that sacramental house
sanctified by holy water and her.

MAKING ENCHILADAS

We set up an assembly line.
I heat the tortillas in manteca
after Crystal dips them in chile ancho
and drains them. Niles carries full plates
of hot tortillas to his father,
who rolls them around spoonfuls of filling.
When we've finished the hot, greasy work,
I pour the last of the sauce over neat rows
of stuffed tortillas, sprinkle them with cheese,
clean the stove and counters.
The kids help their father rinse plates and pans.
They don't know this is the last time.

The cheese melts. Crystal
dances to "No More Lonely Nights" on the radio.
Niles and his dad joke and wrestle.
After grace, we sit before steaming plates.
The kids stuff their mouths, insult each other,
and laugh. We can't avoid their eyes
forever. Their father and I stare
at each other across the table.

THE THINGS SHE GAVE ME

For Juana (Jenny) Gomez Rodriguez

I remember the faces of my children on summer evenings
when their abuela cried, "Don't leave this yard, niñitos,
or La Llorona will get you!"
Eyes huge with horror, they stared into the twilight
like two featherless owls, those harbingers of death.

¡Ay! La Llorona, the woman in white,
wandering the night in tears for the children she drowned,
looking for new little victims.
Everyone in the family had encountered her ghostly figure
or heard her wails one night or another.
More than once, I'd glimpsed her
vanishing from the corner of my sight.

Who was more terrified of such a murderous mother,
my little daughter and son or me, too young,
loving them so, but struggling to find or make a self
among the twisted cords of demands?

My own mother shared common ground with La Llorona,
for neglect and coldness are a kind of death
to the heart of any child. Could this struggle turn me
into ice against my own little ones?
Like them, I turned my eyes to Jenny,
born Juana in Jalisco,
mother to more than their father and tios.

When I married her youngest, we found each other,
the woman with only sons and the girl with no real mother.
She called me hija, taught me things she'd longed to teach
a daughter, the secrets of making killer enchiladas
and pozole, how to comfort child or man
without weakening either,
how to pray the rosary and make a novena.

With Jenny as model, how could I fear the night
and La Llorona's wailing? She showed me how to live
so that those cords couldn't cut yet never broke.

Still, I came to understand grief that sent you
roaming the nights forever when Jenny finally slipped away,
leaving such a hole in the world
that surely none could survive. We did,
as we have a habit of doing, but she remains with me,
after all, in the things she gave me.

The pewter plate engraved with Our Lady of Guadalupe
on my kitchen wall, the cast-iron placa
on which I make tortillas (or used to),
the big lavastone metate her mother carried
crossing the border, along with the cutting
of night-blooming cereus whose descendants thrive
in my windowsill garden. Jenny lives on in the heart
she taught me to use instead of protecting.

I live another life now, but on rare summer nights
I can hear the sounds of weeping in the darkness
or see a wisp of white at the side of my vision
while I'm walking the dog who stiffens and growls
at nothing. La Llorona, go in peace. After all,
the only thing that separates us
is that best of women
and all the things she gave me.

P.O.W.

I

Before I fall into the past,
I drive to the library,
thumb open a book
about the death of a child
in Greenwich Village and
plunge
back
in
time
to trash-filled rooms smelling
of milk, urine, beer and blood,
doors locked and curtains drawn
against the world,
dirty baby brother caged in a playpen,
mother nursing broken nose,
split lip, overflowing ashtray,
and father filling the room to the ceiling,
shouting drunken songs and threats
before whom I tremble and dance,
wobbly diversion, to keep away
the sound of fist against face,
bone against wall.

The book never shows
the other little brothers and sister hiding
around corners and under covers,
but I know they are there
and dance faster,
sing the songs that give him pleasure,
pay the price for their sleep
later, his hand pinching flat nipples,
thrusting between schoolgirl thighs,
as dangerous to please as to anger
the giant who holds the keys
to our family prison. Mother
has no way to keep him from me,
but I can do it for her and them.

Locked by these pages
behind enemy lines again
where I plan futile sabotage
and murder every night,
nine-year-old underground,
I read the end.
Suddenly defiant, attacked,
slammed into a wall,
sliding into coma, death
after the allies arrive,
too late, in clean uniforms so like his own
to shake their heads at the smell and mess—
the end I almost believe,
the end that chance keeps at bay
long enough for me to grow and flee,
my nightmare alive on the page.

Freed too late,
I close the book,
two hours vanished,
stand and try to walk
to the front door on uncertain legs
as if nothing were wrong.
No one must know.
I look at those around me
without seeming to,
an old skill,
making sure no one can tell.
Panic pushes me to the car
where the back window reflects
a woman, the unbruised kind.

In the space of three quick breaths
I recognize myself,
slam back into adult body and life,
drive home repeating a mantra,
"Ben will never hurt me—
All men are not violent,"
reminding myself to believe the first,
to hope for the last.

II

Years later, my little sister will sleep,
pregnant, knife under her pillow,
two stepdaughters huddled
at the foot of her bed,
in case her husband
breaks through the door
again. Finally,
she escapes
with just the baby.

My daughter calls collect
from a pay phone on a New Hampshire street.
She'll stay in a shelter for battered women,
be thrown against the wall
returning to pack
for the trip back to Missouri,
a week before her second anniversary.

Ana and Kay, who sat in my classes,
Vicky, who exchanged toddlers with me once a week,
Pat and Karen, who shared my work,
and two Nancys I have known,
among others too many to count,
hide marks on their bodies and memories,
while at the campus women's center
where I plan programs for women students
on professional advancement
and how to have it all,
the phone rings every week with calls we forward
to safe houses and shelters.

In my adult life, I've suffered no man
to touch me in anger,
but I sleep light.

GHOSTS

I saw the god in you.
Who knows what you saw in me.
A bull's-eye.
A fish in a barrel.
We lurched along like Dr. Dolittle's legendary beast.

At highest noon,
sun at zenith
in summer's worst heat,
I think of you,
trying to sweat you out of me.

When I tried to leave,
you wouldn't let me.
When I tried to stay,
you wouldn't let me.
You made a ghost of me.

Once you lived on the streets,
no other home, for two hungry weeks.
Once I smashed a lamp
over the head of a Hell's Angel.
Once we trusted each other.

I called you gorgeous.
You called me wonderful.
I called you mean.
I said we brought out the worst in each other.
You called me wrong.

Something in you wouldn't accept love.
You could only want me
when you couldn't have me.
The only way I could keep your love
was to go away forever.

Out of synch with each other,
ghosts of our earlier selves
roam that seaside city.
Tell me, love,
do I haunt you?

I SAID I WOULD GIVE YOU WINGS

I will make them from the cerulean scales of butterflies,
the shine of the sun's rays on falling water,
the sound of cicadas crying their love or loneliness,
the heat radiating from miles of cracked concrete,
the salt in the sweat drying on the softest of my skin,
the improvisational, ever-changing jazz of the mockingbird,
the shade of the widest-spreading, creek-draining cottonwood,
the distant roar of the afternoon traffic on the highway,
the soft nesting churr of the buff-feathered mourning dove,
the ache of sun-scoured blue skies in the tender, naked eye,
the sensuous curve of your mouth as it smiles against its will,
the lazy undercurrent of fan and air conditioner humming,
the slip of pure, clear water, ice-chilled, down the throat,
the first, faint shade of moon in the indigo evening sky,
the fireflies blinking codes of lust and love and generation,
the still, jasmine-scented, moisture-heavy midnight air,
the silky, scarlet, moth-borne touch of my heart's devotion.

And you will leap into the air and soar out of sight,
visiting the planets and stars and distant galaxies
to lose your earth-born, manmade pain.
Under the night sky, I will search for your shadow
in the swooping, feather-lifting flight
of every swallow, nighthawk, and owl.

Let me give you wings.

AFRAID

Dad, I'm afraid.
You're not here,
and I'll be going to school tomorrow.
I know I'm going to get suspended again.
These guys have been pushing this guy
to fight me.
I wish you knew I wasn't provoking him.

Well, this is for when you get home,
rip that thick brown leather belt across my arms,
and ask me what the hell I was thinking.
I know.
My response is always a quivering,
"I don't know."

I was afraid and did what you told me.
You used to say,
"If you show them they can bully you and get away with it,
they'll never stop."

ACROSS THE RIVER I WAIT

I'm in my car thinking,
trying to find answers to problems.
Why?
Why is it when I cross the Missouri river
it's like going to a different country?
On the calm side,
what many refer to as God's country,
I see new roads,
people at clubs without security,
nice cars,
and few police.
When I cross the river
I see many people walking the streets
and police hovering like they are white blood cells
fighting off infection.
I go to Kansas Avenue where the Mexicans dwell.
I don't have my gun on me like I used to
even though I get cold stares.
I drive by the worst spots in Kansas City,
Quindaro and Independence Ave.—
the areas where there is razor wire
on the tops of iron gate fences of area stores
and grass growing longer than knee-high
and trash everywhere.
There are also many factories in these poor areas
polluting our Raza.
The factory owners see Mexicans
as people
that have no voice,
that don't count,
that won't stand up.

I have an urge to get lost,
lose my car and just walk with my people,
fight with them.
What am I doing here?
Living in the suburbs when the war is across the river?
Is this education really preparing me for something great?

I don't feel it.
          I don't feel any different
than when I was living on the other side.
I am aware of what's going on
but just being able to open my eyes
makes me want to turn back to what I was before.
And train my carnales to be smarter.
I know it's not right.
The life of crime won't work anymore.
And the drugs would just cloud my vision.
          And still across the river
                                        I wait...

REASON

I used to call writing a curse
when I would get flooded with stories to write
I was angered
because my voice interfered
with my life.
Now I understand
that I need to nurture the gift;
not disrespect it
for the words can be taken
as fast as the thoughts appear.
So here we go...
            I recently stopped writing
because I was working for a false prophet.
I didn't know what a prophet was at the time
but knew I was being led by the lost.
I knew because I had no longer become the seeker,
I had become the sought
by a smart man
who let money and women with taunting eyes,
a lying tongue
and swift feet running toward evil
rule his family.
To some that know me
these words may strike hard
but I know now
that any man can preach
and slither into your heart
with the ease and grace
of a fish cutting water
but unless he's strong enough to speak Jesus' name,
he's no more than the ashes he'll become.

gang leader to Child of God

I hated those people.
I mocked those bible carrying holy rollers.
I blew weed smoke in their face!
Don't brain-wash me with that trash!
Leave me alone!
Thirty years went by. I thought I was free.

A gypsy poet traveling state to state tormented every night!
Couldn't ever stop and LIVE LIFE.
EVERY WORD WAS A POEM,
EVERY THOUGHT WAS A BOOK
AND EVERY SOUND WAS A SONG.
MY NIGHTS WERE DAYS AND MY DAYS WERE NIGHTS
RELIVING MY PAST OVER AND OVER
UNTIL THE LIES COVERED MY FUTURE
Couldn't stop the cocaine and weed to help me write better!
I felt that demon take over my body when I wrote.
It gave me more power than the cocaine
more depression than when I stopped rolling up that dollar bill.
My arms would be marked up with pen ink.
I knew one day "I" was going to be the next E.A. Poe, Baca or Neruda.
It's a dead end trail.
Those of you who have read my stuff and those of you who write
know what I'm talking about.
I'm here, back in Kansas City Across the River.
I know what I need to do.
It's not writing about my Mexican roots, gang life or being a voice
for the injustices that occur to la Raza in the United States.
I learned you can't fight hate with hate.
I've been bought with a price.
Now I sit at the defense for the Gospel of Jesus Christ.
And now it's about giving honor to God
who allowed me to lay down my pen and pick up my sword
and lift up my ink stained arms to worship Him
for washing me with His blood and giving me a clean life
free from weed, cocaine, gangs and war.
Now I write about my God and His Glory
Now I have been made free! Acts 2:38
Thank you Jesus Christ.
King of Kings Lord of Lords

No one knew.

At birth his tiny heart was replaced with a rabbit's heart.
Exotic and furious
beats resonate
as the rabbit heart snuggles in his chest.

Large clouds form letters into words that are ignored.
Shivering monarchs migrate clockwise
as weeping icons wave.

But the hand that touches another
senses fear
and possibilities.

Pragmatic men
motionless
prefer sickness to the cure.

And five drunken writers
collapse in a heap of jumbled words
only to hold their heart
and wonder what happened.

THE THREE MARIAS

The three Marias
dance in crinolines in front of the
black and white television
on a Saturday night.

Far from fiestas and grandparents,
they grow up unloving their brown hearts.

When strangers ask the children, “Do you speak Spanish?”
    Maria A. makes a fist and demands, “Who wants to know?”
    Maria T. replies, “I’m from Pakistan”
    Maria C. pulls letters from the air and pretends to be deaf.

Peanut butter on tortillas and
Herb Alpert on vinyl make the sisters laugh.

Halloween takes them to homes they admire;
homes with central air
doorbells with lights
and driveways with cars that run.

The sisters make a pact;
    Maria A. will collect furniture for sunrooms on the lake,
    while Maria T. practices handshakes with contempt,
    Maria C. resolves to raise a child who understands
    the language of her great grandparents.

The Marias declare love to men whose names are easily pronounced.
And they bear latte-colored children
who astound friends
by eating the hottest salsa
their Abuela can make.

Adios Barbie

Adios Barbie and your
blonde, flat-ass, tortilla-less world.

The closest you ever came to being a Latina,
was your stint as Malibu Barbie
golden as a basted turkey.

Girl, by the looks of you,
I can tell you never had
chicharrones
or
elotes con crema
washed down with eSprite.

Sure you have big chi chi's,
but the lack of meat on your bones
wouldn't flavor Abuela's pot of beans.

And what about your family, güera?
One sister, Skipper, is it? Skipper?
Why not call her,
Maria Paloma Con Queso
or
Conchita Misquita?
At least throw in some cousins;
cousins to ride in cars with
listening to music,
or
cousins whose truck you borrow to pickup
unwanted furniture from your other cousins.

I have to admit—I love the cars you own.
Never once did your cars sit on blocks with
Ken underneath cussing.
Those well tuned machines never left
pools of oil in the driveway
or had to be jump-started.

And how is it you got all those good jobs, like,
doctor, teacher, astronaut¿
Cómo se dice en español—DANG
Why not consider, housekeeper, roofer, nanny?
Fry cook Barbie in a hairnet, I would buy that
or
raggedy, broken down
"Mija take my disability check and cash it!" Barbie.
That would be good!

Well
til you become real with yourself, and stop acting so damn
importante-tudinal, I say,

Adiós Barbie!!

WINDOWPANE

Girls make out
with the boys who are forbidden and convincing.
They know what it's like to run through cornfields in Kansas.
Naked
On acid

And the last names of the boys we loved
we attached to our own
scribbled over and over

till all the names cover thousands of
notebooks and papers
that end up in landfills the size of tiny men nations.

Suppose you love men so much
that you begin thinking like them?
As one lover leaves, another replaces him.
The function of doors.

Petroglyphs in Chaco Canyon are really
ancient porn symbols that translate to; "Yoo Hoo!!"
Like drinks that arrive at your table, "Yoo Hoo!!"

Trees blink with tiny electrical bugs that live to mate.
The man of the house thinks it's funny to mimic
patterns with the porch light; off and on, off and on,
thus endowing himself the biggest light.

The limping professor who swears he's Buddhist,
pays literary tribute to women he has loved.
In his ancient heart.
desire and memories
suffer in prose (or his right hand).

A woman I know
once wore sunglasses on a plane
and pretended to be deaf to avoid contact,
till the end of the flight when
she leaned over the cockpit
and thanked the pilot for the ride.

ELEVEN FOUND DEAD IN A RAIL CAR IN RURAL IOWA

The fragile, scarlet tips of the bushes
quiver in the chilling, October winds

A distant airplane sounds otherworldly
in the dreamless, black print smudges of sky

There is no consolation: no, only
a flightless, bird-like misery pervades

Only their fears, hallucinations strike,
only dehydration and boiling blood

Only visions, the image of their children
reaching for their hands, only emptiness

Out of my insomnia, a lone crow
slowly flaps (receding) into my psyche

On the front steps, a withered jack-o-lantern
grimaces, inconsolably, back at us

THESE SAD DAYS OF SNOW MELTING INTO RAIN

(For my father, dying)

1. Car Radio: Jazz Station Blues

until the final trumpet laughs,
 a jazzy/bluesy refrain whys,

 until the upright bass resounds
more akin to the human heart,

until the tinkling symbols echo
 sharply with the rap of seconds

2. Departure: Terminal Heart News

No, you will never be the same,
 never walk, or remember me,

 or the long family tree bending
under the swiftly melting snow

flailing against the parting breezes
 into the finest, slanting drops

3. Destination: Is The Journey

In the hospital, one more flight,
 and I will reach the last landing,

 then wait until the pink streetlights
shriek like cicadas, insanely,

while we watch their alien eyes
 closely examine mortality

MADRE DE LOS CAMPOS

He wasn't good enough to look at her
but at the end of each week she'd wear a smile
that apologized for her skin.

He'd to talk to her in a way that tried to diminish her.
He'd cheat her out of wages we'd earned with sweat.

Returning to the hot station wagon,
she'd hand everyone their money.
She'd pay herself last with what was left over.

Sitting next to her as she drove everyone home, I seethed.
I hated her for letting him talk to her that way
and for giving away our money to those lazy cabrones
who didn't work as hard
and who didn't pack their lunches or even bring water.

I'd cry hot, angry tears that plowed the dirt on my face.
I vowed never to be as stupid as her.

When she'd drop the last person home,
she'd pull out the egg and chorizo burritos she made us
early that morning for lunch that day.
It was her lunch that she hadn't eaten.

And as my sisters and I shared mom's comida,
she'd give me a smile that apologized for hurting me
but not for loving me.

And I did the same.

SANGRE DE MI PADRE

He smelled like fresh blood
and within moments so did the house.
Long showers couldn't wash away its pungent,
metallic stench or the images from his mind.
The scorching water simply convinced him that he was home.

Mom lit candles to mask the odor
or thank la Virgen for his safe return.
I'm not sure which.
But soon the house smelled like thick warm wax,
sweetly-salted blood and perfumed roses.

I stared at the box of meat he dropped on the kitchen table
knowing he sliced it off the bone of the living hours earlier.
Why didn't the meat drip like the packages
in the case at the grocery store?
Maybe it didn't know it was dead yet.

Mom quickly put his clothes in the washer.
Once, when she threw his clothes in with mine,
I opened the lid to watch my socks and chones turn pink
then the dryer turned them grey.

He'd come out of the shower smelling of Ivory soap—and blood.
His unscarred hands easily reached for a beer as mom
sorted and cooked the fresh meat.
His friends' hands couldn't open refrigerators much less
pull tabs or twist off bottle caps.
We knew there'd come a day
when the blood he'd wash off would be his.

On Fridays, during Lent, he'd bring home fried fish
along with another box of meat.
He'd shower using baking soda instead of soap.
Standing beside him in church as we sang "De Colores,"
I thought about how long it took him to smell like my dad again
and how sad it was that he'd have to start all over on Monday.

CONJURO

Conjuro de ángeles, demonios y duendes que hacen que la Tierra se
desgarre,
que el aire gima y grite entre los árboles
Conjuro de dioses y demonios que hace que mis pensamientos vibren

¡Oh fuerza bruta! Implacable que suena y sacude cada rincón de la Tierra
Temblores internos, temblores externos que se hacen uno y quiebran
la tierra

Hoy te conjuro para que despiertes del letargo que te mantiene cautiva
Hoy invoco al norte, sur, este y oeste
Hoy te conjuro ... a ti guardiana de mi sueño

A la canción de cuna que se oye a lo lejos
A la seguridad ilimitada que me cobija
Al origen de mi sangre, de mi vida, de mi dolor
A la protección que sobrepasa mis necesidades
A la guardiana de mis sueños de las noches más oscuras
Conjuro tu nombre, aquí en mis pensamientos

Spell of angels, demons and elves causing the Earth to tear
making the air howl and scream among the trees
Spell of gods and demons making my thoughts vibrate

Oh brutal strength! Unrelenting strength that resonates and shakes each corner of the Earth
Inner quakes, external quakes that unite and crack the Earth

Today I call on you to wake from your deep slumber that keeps you captive
Today I invoke north, south, east and west
Today I cast a spell on you ... on you, keeper of my dream

To the lullaby that is heard from far
To the endless safety that shelters me
To the origin of my blood, of my life, of my pain
To the protection that overflows my needs
To the keeper of my dreams of the darkest nights
Here in my thoughts, I put a spell on your name

MUJER

Palabra que se disuelve entre los labios
Encantamiento de los bosques con sus aromas más exquisitos
Viento suave que toca el alma
Susurro de dioses que encanta mi razón

Fertilidad ilimitada, vida llevas
Fuerza interminable, rugido de león
Seda exótica de la tierra de mis sueños
Colores cálidos, fríos, combinados

Rayo de sol que atraviesa el árbol que miro
Pájaro que se posa en la copa del sauce
Pasos inaudibles que alcanzan mi alma
Camino de piedras que lleva al río

Vuelo de duendes atravesando la noche
Trueno de fuerza que parte los corazones
Respuesta que calma al hombre más solo
Hombros que soportan las cargas más pesadas

Rayo de luna
Vientre fértil que devora y da vida
Hoja que cae con el otoño
Manos que peinan, manos que hornean, manos que limpian

Voz silenciosa que soporta
Pensamiento creativo, pensamiento desviado, pensamiento guardado

Sombra de burdel
Vientre abultado, fuerte
Noche de tormenta
Cadera agresiva, sexo que hipnotiza.

Puño ensangrentado, puño levantado
Mano de la caricia más experta
Dadora de placer

Entre que lucha por ser escuchado

Bruja guerrera
Diosa, mortal,
Amante, madre; amiga, enemiga,
Dueña, esclava,
Miedo, fe; noche y día.
Hoy y siempre, mujer

MUJER

Word that dissolves between lips
Enchantment from the forest with the most exquisite aromas
Soft wind that touches the soul
Whisper from gods that charms my reason

Endless fertility, carrier of life
Never ending strength, roar of the lion
Exotic silk from the land of my dreams
Colors warm, cold, combined

Ray of the sun that traverses the tree I see
Bird that poses on the top of the willow tree
Inaudible steps that reach my soul
Path of stones that leads to the river

Flight of duendes crossing the night
Thunder of strength that splits hearts
Response that calms the loneliest man
Shoulders that bear the heaviest loads

Ray of the moon
Fertile womb that devours and brings life
Leaf that falls in autumn
Hands that comb, hands that bake, hands that clean

Silent voice that tolerates
Creative thought, deviant thought, stored thought

Shadow of the brothel
Protruding stomach, strong
Stormy night
Aggressive hips, sex that hypnotizes

Bloody fist, raised fist
Hand of the most expert caress
Giver of pleasure

Being who fights to be listened to
Warrior witch
Goddess, mortal
Lover, mother; friend, enemy
Owner, slave
Fear, faith; night and day
Today and always, mujer

ABOUT THE LATINO WRITERS COLLECTIVE

The Latino Writers Collective is a group of Latino writers living and working in the Kansas City metropolitan area. The Collective helps hone and polish the work of its members for publication. In addition to creative support, the Collective organizes and coordinates projects for the larger community, such as the Primera Página and Segunda Página Reading Series, to showcase national and local Latino writers and provide role models and instruction to Latino youth. The mission of the Latino Writers Collective is to foster an environment where the voices of Latino students, blue collar workers, professionals, and homemakers can finally be heard, contributing their experience and vision to the larger community.

Find out more at www.latinowriterscollective.org.

ABOUT THE CONTRIBUTORS

GLORIA MARTINEZ ADAMS is a southwestern Chicana, transplanted in the Midwest. "I belong to part of the rebellious generation that broke loose of the segregation imposed on Hispanos in the '50s, '60s and '70s. If 'I Left my Heart in New Mexico' was a song, it would be my song. Although most of my growing-up years were spent in a dusty mining town in Arizona, I was born in an adobe dwelling in New Mexico and spent summers visiting relatives there. That is where my storytelling comes in —life was good simply sitting around a wood burning stove, pine & piñon permeating the air, listening to stories passed down from generations of Spanish settlers. Those tales never grow old for me." She is co-founder of the Latino Writers Collective.

GUSTAVO ADOLFO AYBAR was born in the Dominican Republic but has lived most of his life in the United States. He just graduated from the University of Missouri-Kansas City with degrees in Spanish and English literature. He hopes to pursue an MFA in creative writing and then a Ph.D. in English.

MARIA VASQUEZ BOYD continues exhibiting, painting and illustrating across the country. Some of her works includes murals in Mexico. A graduate of the Kansas City Art Institute, Boyd later returned to teach in the Design/Illustration Department. She taught at the Nelson-Atkins Museum, worked for Hallmark Cards, and currently is the gallery coordinator for the Guadalupe Center and for The Writers Place. Boyd continues to write poetry and is co-founder of the Latino Writers Collective.

XÁNATH CARAZA is a traveler, educator, and short story writer. She has a Certificate for Overseas Teachers of English from Cambridge University, UK. Having attended graduate school at the School for International Training, she spent three years in Vermont. She also received an MA in Romance Languages and Literatures from the University of Missouri-Kansas City. She has published her original work and essays in *El Cid, La revista estudiantil del Capítulo Tau Iota de Sigma Delta Pi, La Sociedad Nacional Honoraria Hispánica*, and *Utah Foreign Language Review*, University of Utah. The anthology *Más allá de las fronteras, Ediciones Nuevo Espacio*, published an award-winning short story of her work in 2004. She has published in Mexico in newspapers a number of times. She also presented at the X Congreso de Literatura Mexicana Contemporánea in El Paso, Texas, and the Twenty-Ninth Annual Meeting of the Missouri Philological Association.

JOSÉ IGNACIO CARVAJAL REGIDOR was born in San José, Costa Rica. He began writing poetry and attending workshops at a young age. He moved to Lawrence, Kansas in 2002. Ignacio attended the University of Kansas after transferring from Johnson County Community College. He now lives in Austin, where he is working on his graduate studies. Ignacio has been a member of the Collective since 2009.

ANGELA CERVANTES is the author of a short story published in *Chicken Soup for the Latino Soul*. She has been a featured poet for the Riverfront Reading Series and Kansas City's Women Writers Series. Angela is co-founder of the Latino Writers Collective. Angela may be reached at www.angelacervantes.net.

MARIO DUARTE is a graduate of the Iowa Writers' Workshop and the University of New Hampshire. A resident of Iowa City, Iowa, Mario is a long distance member of the Latino Writers Collective. He has published poems in the American Poetry Review, Bryant Literary Review, Broken Plate, Carolina Quarterly, Eclipse, languageandculture, Palabra, Rockhurst Review, Shadowbox, Sycamore Review, Slab, and Steel Toe Review, among others.

JOSÉ FAUS received degrees in Studio Art and Creative Writing from the University of Missouri-Kansas City. José is a muralist with public works locally and in Mexico where he has headed up groups of artists working on public art projects. For José, art is a way to express an interior dialogue—in other words, he talks to himself a lot and sometimes he listens. He reads anything available, especially in waiting rooms. José is a newspaper editor and co-founder of the Latino Writers Collective.

JUANITA SALAZAR LAMB grew up in a bilingual, bicultural family along the Texas border. Her fiction and essays have appeared in Zopilote, Latina Magazine, Border Senses, and Azahares, UA Fort Smith's Spanish-language creative literary journal. She is currently working on a novel.

GABRIELA N. LEMMONS was born and raised in South Texas, a stone's throw from El Rio Grande, and studied with Sandra Cisneros. "As an only child of migrant workers, I was raised in a household where Spanish was the spoken language. My father was a remarkable storyteller and after his passing, I was inspired to write down his recollections. I enjoy writing bilingual poetry and memoir. I am inspired to write so that my only child, Javier, will one day read about the abuelitos he never met. But most importantly, I write so that I may never forget where I came from." She is co-founder of the Latino Writers Collective.

MIGUEL M. MORALES has learned to embrace his beginnings as a migrant farm worker/child laborer in Texas. Today as a student, he employs traditional, nontraditional, and emerging media to help people tell their stories. Miguel is an award-winning journalist most notably earning the Society of Professional Journalists' 2006 First Amendment Award. He serves on the Latino Writers Collective board and is featured in anthology, "Cuentos del Centro: Stories from the Latino

Heartland." Miguel's work also appears on the premier Latino Literature website: La Bloga, in "From Macho to Mariposa: New Gay Latino Fiction," and the forthcoming "Joto: An Anthology of Queer Ch/Xicano Poetry."

JENNIFER PRADO is a graduate student, wife, and brand-new mother. "I'm a small town girl who became closer to her 'Brownness' during college years. La cultura has always tugged at my heart and moved my soul. Above all I hope to bring a genuine and sometimes simple perspective. If I inspire a few people along the way, or remind them of their own familia, it makes my work even more fulfilling."

TOMÁS RILEY is a Chicano artist and activist whose work has been published in several anthologies including *Bum Rush the Page: A Def Poetry Jam.* His first book, *Mahcic*, was published by Calaca Press. Riley's writing career began officially in 1994 as a member of the seminal Chicano spoken-word collective, The Taco Shop Poets (TSP). Blending live music with performance poetry in a style that tipped its hat to collectives like the Last Poets and The Watts Prophets, TSP took on the new power structure engaging California ballot initiatives like Propositions 187, 227 and 209. The group published an anthology and released a CD, both entitled *Chorizo Tonguefire*, to excellent reviews that signaled their arrival as new poetic voices for what mass media had dubbed, for better or for worse, "Generation Ñ" (the Latino version of Generation X).

ANDRÉS RODRÍGUEZ was born in Kansas City in 1955. He has degrees in English from the University of Iowa, Stanford University, and the University of California-Santa Cruz, and has taught writing and literature at various schools around the country. He is the author of a collection of poetry, *Night Song* (Tia Chucha Press), and a work of literary criticism, *Book of the Heart: The Poetics, Letters, and Life of John Keats* (Lindisfarne Press). His poems have appeared in *The Americas Review, Bilingual Review, Blue Mesa Review, The Cortland Review, Palabra, Valparaiso Poetry Review*, and other journals. His poems have also been included in the anthologies *Currents from the Dancing River* (Harcourt Brace), *Dream of a Word* (Tia Chucha Press), *New Chicano/Chicana Writing* (University of Arizona Press), and *Wild Song* (University of Georgia Press). He is the winner of the 2007 Maureen Egan Writers Exchange Prize for Poetry sponsored by *Poets & Writers*. He lives and works in Kansas City.

LINDA RODRIGUEZ is founder/coordinator of the annual Kansas City Women Writers Reading Series, a founding board member of The Writers Place, and has published poetry and fiction in literary magazines such as T*he Kansas City Star, New Letters, New Letters on the Air, Present Magazine, Potpourri, Plainswoman, Wheelhouse Magazine, Writers Digest,* and *Z Miscellaneous*, as well as several anthologies. Her chapbook, *Skin Hunger* (Potpourri Publications, 1995), was named by *Writer's Digest* as one of the four top poetry chapbooks of the year. She has also published numerous articles for general and scholarly publications, including three articles on Rudolfo Anaya's work in the forthcoming *Encyclopedia of Hispanic Literature*. Her cookbook, *The "I Don't Know How to Cook Mexican" Book* (Adams Media) was published in 2008.

JASON SIERRA grew up in El Paso, Texas and began crossing borders early. Crossing back and forth between Mexico and the United States, and being Mexican-American himself, Jason learned that sometimes borders can be fixed and severe, but oftentimes they are blurry or even non-existent. Jason's cultural hybridity has played out throughout his life as he has spent time living with people of different classes and cultures in the United States, Mexico, Canada, Germany, and the Philippines. The cultures that Jason experienced in these countries, as well as the theme of blurring borders can be found in Jason's art, poetry, and music which are heavily influenced by graffiti, pop art, Mexican folk art, and political comics. Jason uses different mediums of expression, working in commercial art, graphic design, illustration, poetry, and music.

MARCELO XAVIER TRILLO left Park University on a book scholarship given by Jimmy Santiago Baca and sponsored by Wind River Ranch in Watrous, NM. After working on the book, Trillo joined Americorps to work with Baca on writing projects, community projects, and prison writing outreach programs. They toured the country facilitating both guest lectures, and film projects in prisons, detention centers, and community centers. Trillo met his wife Angela (also an ex-gang leader), and moved to California to work on film projects. While in California, he got baptized, and asked Jesus if He would help him take his cigarette smoking habit he had had since the age of nine. After quitting his smoking habit, Trillo received the Holy Ghost according to Acts 2:38. He moved back to Kansas City with his amazingly virtuous wife, and three of the best kids: Jesselina, Paul, and Seraphina. Recently anointed a minister, Trillo has dedicated the last four years to bible theology; he lives for God attending the Life Church of Kansas City under Pastor Stan Gleason. Currently, Trillo is completing his undergraduate in Sociology.

GLORIA VANDO's most recent book of poems, *Shadows and Supposes*, won the 2003 Best Poetry Book of the Year Award from the Latino Literary Hall of Fame and the Alice Fay Di Castagnola Award from the Poetry Society of America. She has won numerous other awards and fellowships. She reads her poem, "Fire," on the 2007 Grammy-nominated CD collection, *Poetry on Record: 98 Poets Read Their Work, 1888-2006* (which features Tennyson, Browning, Walt Whitman, who were recorded by Edison when he invented the phonograph). A Puerto Rican born in New York City, Vando's poems have been adapted for the stage and presented at Lincoln Center and Off-Broadway. She is publisher and editor of Helicon Nine Editions, a small press she founded 30 years ago and for which she received the Kansas Governors Arts Award. In 1992, she and her husband, Bill Hickok, founded The Writers Place, a literary center in Kansas City, where they lived. They now live in L.A.

CHATO VILLALOBOS was born in Los Angeles, California, but has lived in Kansas City, Missouri, most of his life. Chato is a new member of the Latino Writers Collective and has been involved in the performing arts for over 15 years, including acting with the Coterie Theater and as a former folkloric dancer with El Grupo Atotonilco. A Kansas City, Missouri, police officer, Chato's current loves are writing poetry and youth advocacy.

www.ingramcontent.com/pod-product-compliance
Lightning Source LLC
LaVergne TN
LVHW051345080426
835509LV00020BA/3296

* 9 7 8 0 9 8 9 5 8 4 4 0 1 *